THE PROMISE

ISBN 978-1901546-354

Acknowledgements

Scripture taken form the New King James Version.
Copyright 1982 by Thomas Nelson, Inc. Used by Permission. All rights reserved.

St. Matthew Publishing Ltd
1 Barnfield, Common Lane, Hemingford Abbots
Huntingdon PE28 9AX   UK
01480 399098
Email: PF.SMP@dial.pipex.com
www.stmatthewpublishing.co.uk

THE PROMISE

Philip Toft

Contents

Preface

This book gives a clear and concise account of the Acts of the Apostles, showing what the Holy Spirit can do in the life of a believer when given the total freedom of possession of a pure heart that loves God.

Be amazed at the miraculous out workings of the gospel. Be challenged by the courage of the carriers of the gospel. But above all be encouraged and stirred into action as a lost world continues to need the gospel more than ever.

Paul Sparks, *Teacher, youth worker and preacher, Bethel Free Church, Warrington*

I used to be rather puzzled and indeed frustrated by the ending of the book of Acts. Luke's thrilling story of the growth of the early church ends with Paul under house arrest in Rome proclaiming the good news of God's kingdom. The story just doesn't seem to end in a neat and tidy way. Was Paul put to death at this point? Was he set free to continue his ministry to be rearrested and executed at a later date? Bible scholars continue to debate these matters. Eventually I realized that Luke has deliberately left the story open ended because the story of the growth of the church continues to the present time. The story will only end with the coming of Jesus.

Acts is a thrilling account about what the risen Christ continued to do through His church in the power of His Spirit. Church growth happens when God's people are open to and empowered by the Holy Spirit to be witnesses for Christ. There will be difficulties along the way. All was not plain sailing for these early believers but as the Lord helped them to work through the problems, He granted the growth!

May your heart be stirred as you read this inspiring account and may you realize afresh that this thrilling story continues with you as it does with me.

Richard Inns, *Pastor, Ebenezer Baptist Church, Chester*

We have four Gospels telling us about the life of Jesus, but only one book telling us the story of the early church. We need to read it carefully and prayerfully.

No reader of it can miss the big challenge that Acts presents to today's church!

This book brings out its message in a clear, direct, vigorous and eminently readable way.

Geoffrey W. Grogan, *Former Principal, Bible Training Institute, (ICC.) Glasgow*

Introduction

Dead religion cannot give the right answer to a world that is crying out in need, but divine instruction can! What does the Living Word of God say?

What happened when the Christian church came to birth? What does the future hold for the people of God in the world today? What should we be doing about it? How can we face the tasks around us?

The promise of the Holy Spirit was given to bring power, purity and purpose to the people of God!

May this little book help every reader to understand the truth more clearly and to and hear God speaking personally. When there are many unscriptural practises emerging in so called Christianity it is wise to refer back to the scriptures.

Jesus Christ has a plan for His church that supersedes the limitation of man's greatest imaginations.

.In these days of moral pollution, spiritual deception and aimless distraction, the Saviour of sinners has a present and eternal purpose for every individual life that has been committed to Him.

This living God wants people to know the precious value they have in His sight.

Things that the first Christian Apostles did in Biblical days, were a demonstration of the work of the Spirit of Jesus Christ in and through them. This was not to enhance their personal self esteem, but to honour their Saviour and to make Him known to others.

The same Holy Spirit is still active today and He will continue to meet with people until the day that their eternal destiny is revealed. His power and grace are available for folk who truly seek Him from the depths of their being. If that is the condition of your own heart, God is for you! May the pages of this book help you to know and experience His person and power in your own life! The words that follow do not claim to bring any fresh revelation, but simply a fresh consideration of God's provision for and pattern of the church of Jesus Christ.

Peter, James, John and the other disciples were given the promise of the Holy Spirit. Mary, the mother of Jesus and other women were to receive its fulfilment as well. This promise was not exclusive to those disciples, but for all who God would call by His Word to receive the personal indwelling visitation that He had spoken of.

The Spirit of God will still come and abide in all who receive Him. He will still empower those who desire His fullness.

Luke was a Greek medical doctor, who after hearing and following the teaching of Jesus of Nazareth, realized that his teacher had come from God on a divine mission. He surrendered his will to the discipline of Christ's word and discovered God's power and purpose filling his own life. Then he was inspired to record all that he had witnessed, so that others too, throughout history, could prove the truth of Christ's promise for themselves. Under inspiration, he wrote the Acts of the Apostles.

Jesus appeared to His fearful followers after the resurrection. They had been secretly meeting in an upstairs room in Jerusalem, afraid of what would happen to them if they were discovered by the authorities who had executed Him. Suddenly the risen, living Christ stood in the middle of the room where they were and offered them His peace! They were terrified; They had seen Him die; They had visited His burial place and been involved in the funeral arrangements! The challenge of Christ's next question can only be understood by those who realize that His word has divine power.

'Why are you troubled? Why do doubts arise in your hearts?'

They thought they were in a locked room with a ghost who was speaking to them!

These men were scared stiff!

Jesus immediately reached out for their understanding.

'Touch me. See me. Eat with me. Listen to me!'

'It was necessary for God's Messiah to die and to rise from the dead!'

These things had been prophetically spoken of centuries before, in the Old Testament. God's word had foretold them, but many people who had read the prophesies, didn't understand how they could be possible or why they were necessary. Now a risen Jesus stood before these terrified men in a upstairs room in Jerusalem and spoke God's word to them personally!

He gave them His peace, breathed on them and said, 'Receive the Holy Spirit.'

The same Spirit that was in Christ was to be within them.

They were given a divine commission, a supernatural task, a life transforming message to take into a hostile world.

Jesus had said that repentance and the remission of sin should be preached in His name, beginning in Jerusalem and taken to every nation.

It would take a spiritual power far greater than their own strength to reach out beyond the walls of the room where they had been hidden, limited by self interest and trapped by fear.

These people who had received His Spirit, still needed a boldness to overcome their fear and an enabling to be His witnesses.

But Christ gave them the promise of His Heavenly Father!

'I will send the Promise of my Father upon you! Wait in the city of Jerusalem until you are endued with power from on high.'

This promised empowering of the Holy Spirit has been made available by the risen Saviour to every redeemed member of His church. Today, in obedience to Christ's command, we too can receive Him in His fullness.

Chapter 1
The Promise

The Feast of Pentecost was a celebration of the full ingathering of the barley harvest of the year in the land of Israel. It was one of three main pilgrimages made to Jerusalem. Held seven weeks after Passover it occurred on the traditional date that the law had been given to Moses on Mount Sinai.

The actual day of Pentecost occurred fifty days after Passover, the time during which Jesus had been crucified. The reality of the resurrection had taken the disciples into a realm beyond anything they had ever understood or expected.

For forty days after He had risen, the Lord had taught them about the Kingdom of God and then taken them to the Mount of Olives where He had ascended before their eyes into heaven. Two angelic messengers had stood before them as they stared upwards in amazement.

'Men of Galilee, why do you stand gazing up into heaven? This same Jesus, who was taken up from you into heaven, will so come in like manner as you saw Him go into heaven!'

Then beyond their own astonishment and fear, the angel's message challenged them to remember and obey Christ's instructions.

They had been told to wait in Jerusalem where they would be endued with power to go into all the world and preach the message of God's gift of salvation made available by what Christ had done.

Forty days of teaching by their risen Saviour had been followed by ten days of prayer in an upper room. God was preparing them by His Word and they were preparing their own hearts by spending time in seeking Him. Judas, the betrayer, had been replaced by Matthias. There were twelve recognised apostles once more, the same as the number of the tribes of Israel. Fifty days passed and the day of Pentecost dawned!

One hundred and twenty disciples were gathered in an upper room in the city. They had a unity of purpose and a passionate desire to receive what God had promised to them. No longer were they scheming and bickering about who should be the greatest; they just wanted Jesus! As they were waiting in that upper room for the promise of power from on high, there came a sound like a rushing mighty wind. When earlier the risen Jesus had breathed on them, He had told them to receive His Holy Spirit. Both the Hebrew and the Greek words for 'breath' can be used for 'spirit.' Now that breath of the Spirit of God had become like a hurricane! It's power filled the whole building where they gathered. Flaming tongues that looked like fire came down upon each one of them, but this was no firework display - The fire that came down from heaven wasn't for their entertainment!

The holy fire of God had been seen by Moses in the wilderness many centuries before. He had been watching the sheep in his father-in-law's flock when he had seen a bush that was growing in the desert; alight, but not being consumed by the flames. The tongues of fire kept leaping heavenward, but the bush wasn't burnt. Going over to investigate he heard God's voice telling him to take off his shoes in reverence, because he was in a holy place, in the very presence of the Lord.

At this burning bush Moses was commissioned to lead the people of Israel out of slavery in Egypt and into a land that the Lord had promised to give them. The fire of God's presence and the command of God's word gave Moses life a significance that the Pharaoh of Egypt could never have given him.

The Children of Israel were led through the wilderness towards this promised land by a pillar of cloud during the daylight hours and a pillar of fire by night. These remained above the tabernacle. They were a manifestation of the 'Shekinah glory of God' that was revealed over the Ark of the Covenant as the Levites carried it ahead of the people and God took the nation forward.

This same fire that Moses had seen at the burning bush, blazed at Mount Sinai when God's law was transcribed on tablets of stone to give to the people who were waiting in the desert below. A divine word,

12

accompanied by this holy fire called them to become a new nation, living according to God's order. The tragedy was that they failed!

Six centuries later, the prophet Elijah stood on Mount Carmel, in the promised land and issued another challenge to the gathered people.

'If the Lord is God, follow Him, but if Baal, follow him!'

With this prophetic challenge, the people of Israel were given a stark choice. They were in danger of completely loosing their God given identity and purpose. They had been called to demonstrate the banner of fulfilled prophesy. At the appointed time the divine Messiah would come out of their nation, into the world, by a Jewish virgin who would bear a Son. One of His titles would declare His divine identity, 'God with us!'

'Baal' was the Canaanite fertility god, who endorsed gross immorality and demanded child sacrifice.

The choice that the ancient people of Israel had to make is still relevant in the selfish, pleasure seeking, amoral, abortion ridden societies that prevail in the world today! Without people realizing it, these standards that oppose God's law are inspired by the enemy of their own souls.

Elijah challenged the prophets of Baal to build an altar on Mount Carmel upon which to make a sacrifice. After they had placed wood upon it to make a burnt offering, they had to call upon their god to send fire from heaven. No natural means of combustion had to be used. Elijah would do the same to his God, Yahweh, the God of Israel. The God who answered by fire was the true God!

The frenzied prophets of Baal slashed themselves with knives in frantic endeavour to get an answer from their pagan deity, but it was all to no avail. When it was Elijah's turn he ordered twelve barrels of water to be poured on the alter. Perhaps this spoke symbolically to the twelve tribes of Israel. Certainly it was a very bold thing to do when the drought had made water so precious. The sacrifice and the wood were soaked, but God, the eternal God, answered His prophet's prayer. The fire of heaven consumed the sacrifice and in the judgment that followed, the prophets of Baal were slain. Then there came a time of great spiritual and moral purification when the nation returned to worship the living God.

Forty days after the resurrection, the Lord Jesus ascended in a cloud from the Mount of Olives and the fire of the Holy Spirit came down at Pentecost. He went up into the cloud and the fire came down from heaven. The fire of the Holy Spirit comes with refining power! When the purifying fire of God fell upon the disciples of Christ, the life of heaven had come down! The life of Christ was within them! They were filled with the Spirit of God, the Holy Spirit, the Spirit of Jesus their Saviour and they began to speak in other tongues. Languages that they had never learned began to pour from their lips in glorious testimony of the greatness of what God had done through His Son! It was holy and it was powerful. This was not simply praying in 'tongues,' it was making a proclamation to all the world.

Jews and proselytes from every nation, heard in their own dialects, the disciples declaring the wonderful things that God was doing.

Pentecost was a time of tremendous proclamation, but the whole city was amazed and perplexed! 'What could this mean?' – What is this?

Peter, the fisherman who had been called and equipped to be an Apostle, a messenger sent from Christ, gave them the answer.

'This is what was spoken by the prophet Joel: And it shall come to pass in the last days, says God, that I will pour out my Spirit on all flesh.'

It was not just for apostles, priests and prophets, but in God's mercy, because of the new covenant that He had made by the blood of His Son, the promise was available for all who came in faith to Christ.

'Your sons and daughters shall prophesy, your young men shall see visions; your old men shall dream dreams.'

As Peter continued his message, it was no ear tickling, socially pleasing, exhibition of political correctness! He went through Scriptures that many of them would have known, bringing an interpretation that challenged them to the very depths of their souls.

'God has made this Jesus, whom you crucified, both Lord and Christ.'

'Christ' was not a surname, it was the title of the anointed Messianic messenger of God.

The Scriptures had been fulfilled in Jesus, but many had rejected Him!

People listening to Peter heard his message and they were cut to the heart.

When God's Word is cutting, its purpose is to save life! It is divine surgery!

'What shall we do?' Many of these people had done plenty. They had tried to be good. They were in Jerusalem for the religious feast of Pentecost. They tried to keep the Mosaic law, but they had rejected Christ in His earthly ministry. They knew that they did not have a saving faith! Even with all of their good works, they did not have a living relationship with God and because of their own sin they were abhorrent in His sight!

The same diagnosis remains today. Almighty God cannot have fellowship with sinners. Sin makes even the most self righteous of us repulsive to Him; But still He loves us! This is why He dealt with the death penalty of sin. The Word of God speaks of the way of salvation in Christ! The Almighty Father sees all who receive His Son as their Saviour in the light of the price that Jesus paid for their forgiveness at Calvary. The blood of one who was not only the Son of Man, but the Son of God had been shed to make it possible. There was no other way it could have happened.

Peter gave God's answer to the desperate inquiry of those seeking people on the day of Pentecost.

'Repent and be baptised in the name of Jesus Christ for the remission of sins and you shall receive the gift of the Holy Spirit; for the promise is to you and to your children, to all who are afar off, as many as the Lord our God will call!'

On the day of Pentecost the spiritual fruit from that first harvest amounted to three thousand people being saved for eternity!

Almighty God is still saving people! True faith in Jesus Christ is still bringing men and women into a place of peace with God. The Holy Spirit is still filling men and women with the power to witness for Jesus. They are not called to go and 'do some witnessing,' they are empowered to be witnesses by the evidence that God has saved them from lives of sin and self-centredness. True Christians are called to be living witnesses! As we individually respond, this salvation is personal to each one of us. The Lord Jesus Christ is the God of our salvation!

When Peter challenged his listeners to 'Be saved from this perverse generation,' the lives of the folk who received his message were transformed.

Transformed, not reformed. The Holy Spirit had worked in them. Hearts and homes were opened for God to use. There was a concern for others and a care for one another. They went to one another's houses and listened to scripture being taught. They had fellowship with each other. They broke bread and remembered what the Lord Jesus had said on the night of the last Passover feast,

'This is my body which is given for you; Do this in remembrance of Me. This cup is the new covenant in my blood, which is shed for you.'

Remembering Jesus in this way was to become a celebration of eternal significance. They would have remembered the prophesies of the Messiah's coming and of how Jesus had fulfilled all that the old testament had said about Him. They would have remembered their Saviour's presence with them, of the miracles He had done and the teaching He had given. They would have remembered the promise they had received that He would return again and they would have worshipped Him as the mighty God of their salvation.

They prayed together in a way that was far greater than any religious ritual they had known and they saw God send answers!

Spiritual gifts continued to demonstrate Christ's presence and power in the early church.

The presence and power of God have never diminished! Both fear and joy filled the lives of those early believers, as in simplicity of faith and gladness of heart, they worshipped the Lord in the power and fullness of the Holy Spirit. Their fear was not one of unhealthy terror but of reverent respect. The fear of the Lord was foundational in their faith. They saw that God was still working miracles and they gladly heard His word. Every day more and more people gave their lives to Jesus!

Chapter 2
Walking, Leaping and Praising God

The life of God was so manifestly in His people, that not only were they blessed, but through them, others saw their own need of salvation. Christ's presence was not in conjuring tricks, psychosomatic healings and pseudo prophesies.

The promise of God's power was real and the purpose of that power was to see men and women saved for eternity because of what Jesus had done at Calvary.

At three o'clock in the afternoon Peter and John walked together to a prayer meeting in the temple in Jerusalem. God had spoken through Isaiah the prophet hundreds of years before Christ was born and stated,

'My house shall be called a house of prayer for all nations.'

However when Jesus had gone to the temple in the last days of His earthly ministry some eight weeks previously, He had added to the quote from the prophet when He had said to the traders within its walls,

'My house is a house of prayer, but you have made it a den of thieves!'

Now Peter and John were walking past one of the entrances to the temple which was called, 'The Beautiful gate.' Its large and ornately designed structure, separated the women from the gentile people who gathered in different courtyards.

Outside the gate sat a man who had been crippled from infancy. He was begging.

He hoped to receive charitable gifts from people passing by on their way to worship. The Jewish worshippers coming to the temple would have been more disposed to helping him in this way as they came to bring their own requests to God. When the crippled man saw Peter and John walking past, he called out to them and asked them for alms. Peter stopped in his tracks and looked straight at the man, with the command,

'Look at us!'

He didn't give this instruction to boost his own ego; but to bless the man in the Name of the Lord Jesus.

The lame man returned Peter's gaze, expecting to receive a generous donation. The idea of a miracle of healing would probably never even have entered his mind.

The ministry of these two converted fishermen wasn't focused around finance. They weren't trying to build up their own popularity and they didn't have medical expertise. They were men of prayer and they knew that their Saviour was able to meet this man's need.

'Silver and gold I do not have, but what I do have I give you: In the name of Jesus Christ of Nazareth, rise up and walk!'

As these two Spirit-filled disciples identified with their Lord, they also reached out to identify with this needy man by grasping his right hand and helping him upright. These men of prayer knew that the power of God was real! Immediately the disabled man's lower limbs were strengthened and he leapt to his feet. As the shock of what had happened went through his whole being, he was instantly transformed! Walking, leaping and praising God, he immediately went to the temple to give thanks. Some wag has suggested that he asked for alms and God gave him legs! In reality the power that had raised Jesus from the dead, brought healing to this lame man, who previously could only beg at the roadside for a living. Now his walk was changed both physically and spiritually. He no longer needed to beg at the roadside, he had a new life to live trusting Jesus. His praise to God was absolutely genuine. In answer to the prayer of these disciples, God had touched this man with divine power and then he in turn gave God all of the glory! His life was a living testimony to the risen Saviour.

The spectators who had seen all of this were amazed and ran to Solomon's porch in the temple area to try and understand what was happening. This man had been a beggar for years. He had been handicapped from birth. He had been there when the Lord Jesus had walked the streets of Jerusalem and not been healed, but now, by faith in Christ, the power of the Lord had touched him through Peter and John. When the disciples saw the crowd gathering, Peter began to preach the gospel to the people.

His message challenged their lack of faith.

'Men of Israel, why do you marvel at this?'

He challenged them for being astounded, but immediately declared that it was not his own ability that had worked the miracle: It was the work of God who glorifying His Son Jesus!

He called them to personal responsibility.

'You denied the Holy One and Just and asked for a murderer to be granted to you. You killed the prince of life, whom God has raised from the dead.'

Not another word was spoken about the crippled man who had been healed. No invitations were given to come and have legs lengthened or knees strengthened or anything else. Not everyone of these folk would have been at Calvary on the day Jesus was crucified, but they all needed to understand the personal significance of His death and resurrection. They were guilty of sin and only the sacrifice of Calvary could purchase their forgiveness. The same is true today!

The message Peter preached was about Jesus. It was given fearlessly and in love, pointing to a way of repentance and salvation. The listeners were reminded of the promise of Moses, who had led their ancestors to freedom from slavery in Egypt.

'The Lord your God will raise you up a prophet like me from among your brethren.'

Moses had challenged the people to hear and obey all that this messenger of God would tell them to do.

The title given to the Lord, in Peter's address, was 'God's Servant.' This will have brought to mind the words of Isaiah the prophet, speaking of the messiah who would come as God's 'Suffering servant.'

'He was despised and rejected by men, a Man of sorrows and acquainted with grief and we hid, as it were, our faces from Him; He was despised and we did not esteem Him. Surely He has borne our grief and carried our sorrows; Yet we esteemed Him stricken; Smitten by God and afflicted: But He was bruised for our iniquities; The chastisement of our peace was upon Him and by His stripes we are healed.'

In Christ these prophesies had been fulfilled before their eyes.

Peter declared the truth of God's word and offered the way of refreshing from the presence of the Lord. His proclamation was powerful, pointing to Jesus as the one through whom every family on earth would be blessed. While his address was continuing, temple officials came to see what all the furore was about. When they heard the disciples declaring that Jesus of Nazareth, who they had handed over to be crucified, had now risen and was working miracles, they were angry. The fact that a cripple could walk, was of little concern to them. Their own position was under threat and so they had the preachers arrested. However God's word had already done it's work! Five thousand men came to believe in Christ! The priests, Sadducees and temple security guards opposed the only message that could save the people they themselves should have been serving! Without understanding whose side they were on, these religious officials had aligned themselves against Almighty God. They locked the disciples in prison for the night because they had healed the sick and preached the message of salvation that honoured Christ.

The next day when Peter and John were brought for examination before the dignitaries in Jerusalem they were asked where they got the authority to do what they had done.

Political and religious systems that do not recognise the truth of God's word in the power of Spirit of Christ, will make the same challenges still.

Peter still showed respect to the civil and temple authorities who questioned him, calling them the 'rulers of the people' and 'elders of Israel.' He showed respect, but rather than replying to their questions with deference, he demonstrated that he himself was subject to a higher authority. Filled with the Holy Spirit he answered,

'If this day we are judged for a good deed done to a helpless man, — let it be known to you all and to all the people of Israel, that by the name of Jesus Christ of Nazareth, whom you crucified, whom God raised from the dead; by Him this man stands here before you whole.'

He continued with his challenging response,

'There is no other name given among men by which we must be saved!'

The officials had asked with what authority Peter and John had acted, but when they saw the boldness of these uneducated, untrained men, they realized they had been with Jesus! It is from Him that true Pentecostal authority still comes!

Further threats to silence the disciples brought the response,

'Whether it is right in the sight of God to listen to you more than God, you judge: For we cannot but speak of the things which we have seen and heard!'

As soon as they were freed from their interrogation, they went back to the other believers and told them what had happened. The whole group began to pray with a unity of heart and mind. It was the same unity of purpose that had been there when the fire from heaven had come down on the waiting disciples in the upper room.

Here, just a matter of days later this Spirit empowered cry from their hearts was offered as fresh prayer. They were applying the scriptures to their own situation as they quoted the Messianic psalm written centuries before by King David:

'Why did the nations rage and the people plot vain things,— against the Lord and His Christ?'

Their relationship with God was personal and powerful and the request they made was specific.

'Now Lord, look on their threats and grant to your servants that with all boldness they may speak your Word, by stretching out your hand to heal and that signs and wonders may be done through the name of your holy Servant Jesus!'

As on the day of Pentecost, signs and wonders were not given simply to satisfy a natural fascination with the supernatural. The building where they were meeting began to rock and tremble. The first sign they received in answer to prayer was divine shaking! It wasn't an earthquake, it was a 'God shake.' Divine shaking had confirmed His word in the past. When the Lord had given Moses the law, the commandments at Mount Sinai, the whole mountain had shaken.

Later the writer to the Hebrews said,

'Yet once more I shake not only the earth but also heaven. Now this 'Yet once more,' indicates the removal of those things that are being shaken, as of things that are made, that the things which cannot be shaken may remain.'

Sometimes God allows things to be shaken in order to reveal what sort of a foundation they have.

Jesus had told a parable of a wise man who built his house on a rock and a foolish man who built his without a proper foundation. He then gave the interpretation.

'Whoever comes to Me and hears my sayings and does them, I will show you what he is like. He is like a man building a house who dug deep and laid the foundation on the rock.- The flood arose, the stream beat vehemently against that house and could not shake it, for it was founded upon the rock; But he who heard and did nothing is like a man who built a house on the earth without a foundation against which the stream beat vehemently and immediately it fell and the ruin of that house was great.'

When the storms came, the house on the rock remained and the house without foundations collapsed.

The word of God is a sure foundation in a shaking world. Every person that ever lives here will one day face the storm of death and judgment to follow.

Those early disciples came out of the shaking house and spoke God's word boldly!

It had affected all of their lives. It had changed the way they lived and given them a message to take to others. This little group that had believed in Christ had now become a multitude who cared for one another with a concern that was sacrificial. They recognised that the material possessions they had were God given and that they were only the temporary stewards of them. Whenever there was material need among the believers, support was distributed and nobody lacked anything. This wasn't an early form of communism, it was a demonstration of Christian care. Christ's love was revealed in and through those early disciples in the Roman occupied, religion ridden, mission field where the church had been born. Before His death the Lord had commanded them,

'Love one another as I have loved you, — By this all will know that your are my disciples, if you have love one for another.'

Those early believers in the Lord Jesus not only praised God when a cripple was healed, but also in the face of opposition.

Chapter 3
Deceit, Discipline and Declaration

Joses, a member of the Jewish priestly tribe of Levi, had originally come from the island of Cyprus. The message of the gospel had not only found a place in his heart, but it had affected every part of him.

Peter, John and the other disciples who had been commissioned as apostles, called him by a new name, 'Barnabus.' This name reflected his conversion and his character. It meant 'Son of encouragement.' Under the old Mosaic law, the Levites had not been supposed to own property or land. For many of the Levites, this regulation had fallen into neglect and Barnabus did own land, probably on Cyprus, where he had come from. When he joined the other followers of Christ, he sold his land and gave the money to the apostles for use in the work of the gospel.

His heart was overflowing with the love of God and he was prepared to give generously, in order to share the message of salvation with those around him. Peter, James and John had left their fishing to become 'fishers of men.' Others too had made material sacrifices, demonstrating a Christ-like compassion to all who were connected with the early church. It wasn't long however before this commendable work of God in the hearts of the people had a counterfeit. It has been part of a Satanic strategy throughout history to counterfeit the work and gifts of God with substitutes that are either fleshly or demonic in origin. The church today needs to be more discerning than it ever has been. Speaking prophetically of the last days of world history, the Lord Jesus had warned His listeners that the 'very elect' would be deceived if it were possible.

Ananias and his wife Saphira sold some of their land and gave part of the money it raised to the apostles, but pretended that they had given it all. Perhaps their motive was to gain more credibility among the early believers. Peter confronted Ananias about the source and nature of his dishonesty.

'Why has Satan filled your heart to lie to the Holy Spirit and keep back part of the price of the land for yourself? While it remained was it not your own and after it was sold, was it not in your own control? Why have you conceived this thing in your heart? You have not lied to men but to God.'

Ananias immediately collapsed and died at Peter's feet. God had taken terrifyingly radical measures to ensure that the foundations of the church were built on truth! Saphira came in soon afterwards and was asked if she and her husband had sold the property for the sum that Ananias had lied about. She was party to his dishonesty and as a result she faced the same judgment as her husband.

'The feet of those who buried your husband are at the door and they will carry you out.'

The radical response to Ananias and Saphira's action was not over their generosity, but because God was concerned for the absolute truthfulness of their testimony about His Son. Such measures brought great fear not only to the church, but to all who heard about what had happened. This particular outworking of faith in Christ was not a popular political or a social strategy! The divine discipline of the believers kept their faith pure. Shortly afterwards, through the revelation of New Covenant scripture, the responsibility of maintaining Godly discipline was committed to members of each local assembly of believers who gathered in the name of the Lord Jesus. This certainly did not exclude the sovereign correction of God. He disciplines those whom He loves in order that they may not be deceived by the enemy of their souls. The Lord is very patient with His people, but where there is no discipline of sin, no declaration of absolutes, one must question whether or not it is the true church that is seen. Humanistic teaching that denies sin is totally divorced from the declaration of God's mercy to repentant sinners. His patience is infinite, but the call to holy obedience is personal and those who persistently refuse to repent do not have the Holy Spirit dwelling in their lives. The worst discipline God administers to the living is to withdraw all conviction of sin and hand them over to do just as they choose with no further opportunity of repentance. Only hell awaits them.

After the day of Pentecost, the people who heard all that had happened to Ananias and Saphira feared the Lord. This fear was not an abject terror, but an awesome awareness of a powerful and holy God.

The Psalmist declares, 'The fear of the Lord is the beginning of wisdom; A good understanding have all those who do His commandments.'

The promised work of the Holy Spirit brought purity to the church of Christ. God is eternally holy and He calls His people to be holy.

Crowds came with reverence and respect to hear the gospel preached. Supernatural signs followed it's declaration and confirmed the truth of it's message. Sick people were healed from many different ailments and folk tormented by demonic powers were delivered and set free to worship the Lord Jesus.

Both the decease of Ananias and Saphira and the miracles among the multitudes were mighty demonstrations of the word and work of Christ in the power of the Holy Spirit!

There was a unity of purpose among the apostles that was inspired by the gospel message. It was holy, it was Christ centred and it was powerful. The message of a miracle working, prayer answering Saviour resounded beyond the city of Jerusalem and as a result, people from the surrounding towns came to find out what was happening for themselves. Crowds came to Solomon's porch to hear and see what God was doing.

The very officials who had forbidden Peter and John to preach about Christ, saw with their own eyes the effect of the message! Their own response was rapid, but it wasn't one of delight because of blessing from God. They weren't humbly acknowledging who Jesus was, but responding in jealous antagonism to all that the apostles stood for. These people in authority were indignant.- How dare these fishermen and peasants defy the orders of the political and ecclesiastical hierarchy? To silence them, Peter and John were arrested and thrown into jail, but Almighty God still had a message for them to deliver to the people gathered in the temple area! The cell doors had been slammed and bolted shut, but during the night an angelic messenger came, opened the prison doors and lead the apostles to freedom, with a further instruction to declare God's word.

'Go and stand in the temple and speak to the people all the words of this life.'

With the thrilling courage that had been imparted when they had been baptised in the Holy Spirit, Peter and John went straight back to the temple and continued to preach about Jesus! They knew they need fear nothing else because they feared Almighty God!

The gospel of Christ is the message of eternal life. Even when God's refining judgment had brought death to Ananias and Saphira, He still wanted people to live!

The next morning it was reported to the priests and temple security staff that the officials who had gone to see the apostles had only found a locked and guarded prison cell that was completely empty. The temple officials had no idea what to do. It was possible that they thought that some of the jail staff had released their prisoners, but they could see that the crowds were listening to the disciples preaching in the temple and they were fearful of starting a riot if they re-arrested them. As a result they escorted them to the council with less aggression than previously, but still in total opposition to their message.

'Did we not strictly command you not to teach in this name? And look, you have filled Jerusalem with your doctrine and intend to bring this man's blood on us!'

Satan's opposition to the message of a risen Saviour, was being expressed by those with social responsibility and religious position. All through history the devil has tried to corrupt and silence the gospel, but the life giving declaration of God's word is powerful still!

The fire of the Holy Spirit that came down on the day of

Pentecost was burning in the apostle's hearts and they spoke with divine authority!

'We ought to obey God rather than men. The God of our fathers raised up Jesus whom you murdered by hanging Him on a tree. Him God has exalted to His right hand to be Prince and Saviour, to give repentance to Israel and forgiveness of sins.'

The same Lord Jesus is still empowering people to be His witnesses today!

These early believers discovered that the very circumstances that opposed them brought a further witness of Christ's glory. The things that were against them became tools to further the work of evangelism.

They were not showing disrespect to those in positions of leadership, but showing greater respect to the Lord who had transformed their lives.

Chapter 4
Power and Persecution

The early church not only declared the word of God in the power of the Holy Spirit, but it engaged in good works that demonstrated His love. Those who gathered together in worship were also prepared to show care one for another. Many more people joined with them, but with more people came fresh practical problems. Some were proselytes from a Greek background who had come to Jerusalem for the feast of Pentecost, but after hearing the disciples preaching, they recognised Jesus as their Messiah. A number of them had widows connected to their family. The Hebrew ladies who had lost their husbands were being cared for by the church in Jerusalem, but the widows from the Greek culture were being neglected. Grumbling arose and the apostles sought to deal with it in a Godly way. Their own priority was to spend time in prayer and preaching the Word of God, so when they saw these fresh needs that had to be dealt with, they gave instructions for the choice of seven deacons to take responsibility in the situation.

The deacons were not simply social workers, they were men of wisdom, full of the Holy Spirit who wanted to bring honour to Jesus. Because they were glad to serve these needy folk, their own testimony brought further increase to the numbers of people coming to put their trust in Christ.

Stephen was one of the deacons, full of faith and the power of God and as a result of this, there were miracles confirming his ministry. However instead of this bringing joy to the religious authorities, it brought further jealous opposition.

The Synagogue of the Freedmen was composed of Jews from families that had been slaves in Rome. They themselves had returned to Israel to seek a purer form of Judaism. When they heard Stephen preaching and saw the miracles that accompanied his ministry, they began to argue with him. The anointing of the Holy Spirit upon him gave a wisdom and authority that they could not subdue, so they began scheming against him. False witnesses accused Stephen of speaking against their land of Israel, against the law that Moses had given to their nation and against the temple where they worshipped. These matters were all fundamentally important in the Jewish culture and existence.

When the high priest asked Stephen about the validity of the charges, he didn't even seek to defend himself, but pointed to their own religious history and the challenges that the nation had previously faced when they had been called to move on in their understanding of God's purposes. This gracious and humble man spoke with a passion that had his accusers sitting on the edge of their seats as they listened to him. He spoke of their founding father.

Before Jacob, (who became Israel) was even born, Abram had met God in Ur of the Chaldeas, an advanced civilization in ancient Mesopotamia, now present day Iraq. When God met with him there, Abram was told to leave his city and its culture behind. The inhabitants practised an immoral and superstitious cultic worship of the stars. Abram himself was not a Jew and he did not live in the area that was known as Canaan, but the God who was going to give the land and bless the children of Israel, called their patriarch from outside its boundaries. Abram's obedience to God would bring blessing to the whole world.

'Get out of your country, from your family and your fathers house, to a land that I will show you. I will make you a great nation; I will bless you and make your name great and you shall be a blessing. I will bless those who bless you and I will curse him who curses you and in you shall all the families of the earth be blessed.'

Because Abram was prepared to trust God with his family and his future, he was called the 'friend of God' and even after his own personal failures, the promise was repeated. He became known as the 'father of the faithful' with children of faith not merely limited to his own genetic line, but drawn from every nationality in the world.

Even as Stephen reminded Ananias the High Priest, of Israel's own history, the outworking of what God had promised to Abram was being outworked by Jesus, the great High Priest of the Christian church.

Then Stephen spoke of Joseph, who centuries later became a slave in Egypt. God had not only revealed Himself to him there, but used him mightily. As Joseph approached his own death, he gave instructions to take his remains with his people, when they moved to the land that God had promised to his great-grandfather Abram. His life was a prophetic pointer to Christ.

Stephen continued and reminded the High Priest and his entourage that God had spoken to Moses at Midian. In the wilderness he had heard the divine commission to go and free the children of Israel, who had been slaves in Egypt for four hundred years. They were to move on to the place of promise, which would be a land where they could be at rest. Stephen's sermon was challenging the Jews listening to him to move on from a faith in the land and in their historical culture, to a rest of faith in the Messiah who had been revealed to them.

King Solomon had built a splendid temple in Jerusalem about nine hundred and sixty years before Christ was born. Through the battles of the centuries, it had been held with the utmost esteem in the heart of every believing Jew, but Stephen quoted the prophet Isaiah and reminded his accusers that God did not dwell in houses made by men, but that heaven was His throne and earth His footstool.

Throughout history, the revelation of an unchanging God had been ongoing and He had always used His prophets to challenge His people to move on in faith.

There was nothing uncertain about Stephen's address. It was a clear challenge from God's word, but it was given with such a radical application that his accusers were furious. Their fundamental culture and belief systems were being challenged.

Stephen continued,

'You stiff necked and uncircumcised in heart and ears! You always resist the Holy Spirit; as your fathers did, so do you. Which of the prophets did your fathers not persecute? And they killed those who foretold the coming of the Just One of whom you now have become betrayers and murderers, who have received the law by the direction of angels and have not kept it.'

The Lord had said through Isaiah the prophet,

'On this one will I look; On him who is poor and of a contrite spirit and who trembles at my Word.'

Stephen's listeners didn't tremble at the word, they trembled in anger!

With uncontrolled fury they launched forward to take his life, gnashing at him with their teeth. They dragged him outside Jerusalem and began to stone him.

This spirit-filled deacon's address didn't seem to be the best way to raise money for the building fund, but he knew that almighty God was building His church! His earthly ministry had finished. He saw heaven opened and Christ standing at the right hand of God. As the rocks crashed into his body, his face was radiant and he appealed to a higher authority than the Sanhedrin.

'Lord Jesus, receive my spirit.'

A young man called Saul of Tarsus was there, holding the coats of the men who were throwing the missiles. He was a highly educated Pharisee, with a burning antagonism against the followers of Christ.

Stephen, this deacon who had served God by serving the widows in the church, made his last prayer.

'Lord do not lay this sin to their charge.'

The final words that ever came from the lips of this man were an echo of the words of His Saviour on the cross.

'Father forgive them for they do not know what they do.'

Godly men took his body and grieved over the death of the first Christian martyr. There was great sadness over his loss. On the same day that he was buried, opposition to the Christians became persecution and believers were hounded out of Jerusalem. Throughout history, the persecution of believers has often been at the hands of men who did not even realize they were being used as Satan's tools. Before Jesus had been nailed to the cross, He had warned His disciples,

'You will be hated by all for My name's sake but he who endures to the end will be saved.'

If there is revival without opposition, it's source needs to be questioned. True revival, a real moving of the Spirit of God in the lives of people, has always been accompanied by an opposition inspired by the devil himself.

Through Stephen's ministry the church had literally to move on in the purposes of God. The gospel went across Judea and Samaria and its witness began to spread out into all the world as Christ had commanded. God was still building His church! Jesus had said,

'I will build my church and the gates of Hades shall not prevail against it.'

The horrors of persecution that have occurred throughout the years have produced pain that has almost been unbearable. Physical and psychological torture have been applied to men and women to make them recant their faith in Christ and yet God has sustained them. Some like Stephen, have gone home to a glorious heavenly reward and some have been delivered and been given a stronger message than before. Some have come out of persecution as broken people, with bodies mangled by the inhumanity of man under devilish inspiration, but God has put divine value on them all. The Scriptures say,

'Precious in the sight of the Lord is the death of His saints.'

Martyrs are given an eternal reward. Stephen was welcomed to heaven by the Lord Himself! He would have rejoiced with those whose victory over Satan John of Revelation referred to when he wrote,

'And they overcame him by the blood of the Lamb and by the word of their testimony and they did not love their lives to the death.'

Chapter 5
Counterfeit and Correction

Out of persecution came glorious proclamation. As the disciples were scattered they preached! The challenge of Stephen's death for Christ left them with an even greater passion to live for God.

The work of the Holy Spirit in and through them, was part of God's building program for His church that had been prepared from eternity. It was made possible at Calvary and expressed at Pentecost. The disciples own lives had been laid on the foundation of Christ as the rock of their salvation and they had been used to raise up pillars of teaching, fellowship, communion and prayer among the infant believers. Now they were involved in the extension work.

Philip, another of the deacons who had been chosen to serve alongside Stephen, went to Samaria. Communication between the Jews and the Samaritans had been strained for hundreds of years. This went back to the time when the inhabitants of Jerusalem had been in captivity in Babylon, over five centuries before Christ. The temple and the walls of the city had been destroyed by the Assyrians invasion. People from the region of Samaria had stayed in the land of northern Israel, but began to intermarry with the surrounding nations and accept their gods. As a result the Samaritans became a nation of mixed race and mixed religion.

After seventy years in captivity the inhabitants of Jerusalem were allowed to go back to the city to rebuild the walls and the temple. The Samaritans tried to amalgamate with them and then to stop them. The Jews who had returned from captivity continued to rebuild the broken walls of Jerusalem and reconstruct the temple. These were restored, but as a result, bitter enmity grew up between the Jews and the Samaritans. Ezra the scribe and Nehemiah had declared the need for purity of race and religion. Samaria became forbidden territory for practising Jews. When travelling north they would detour around it rather than take the shorter journey through it. During His earthly ministry Jesus had deliberately walked through Samaria and stopped at the well outside the little town of Sychar, while the disciples who were with Him went to get some food. As He sat at the side of the well, a woman came there to draw water. It was noon, the hottest time of the day and she was alone. The women of the town normally came when it was cooler. She had chosen to come alone because of the turmoil her life was in. When Jesus saw her He asked her for a drink. This astounded her. She knew that the Jews had nothing to do with the Samaritans and she wanted to know what His motives were.

Jesus answered,

'If you knew the gift of God and who it is who says to you, 'Give me to drink,' you would have asked Him and He would have given you living water.'

She didn't understand that He was speaking about the Spirit of God, but something within her wanted what He was referring to.

'Give me this water so that I don't thirst and have to come here.'

Jesus had answered her, 'Go, call your husband .'

He knew she had no real husband and had lived with five different men before her current partner.

She was thirsting for love and in her search she had only made more enemies.

The words Jesus spoke to her had cut into her heart like a surgeons knife. He was indeed like a surgeon, but His word was not spoken to humiliate her, but to operate on the cancer of sin that was destroying her life. When He told her what He saw in her, she immediately tried to change the subject and begin a religious argument, but Jesus would have none of it. He had not come to argue about religion, but to enable her to establish a pure and personal relationship with the living God.

'True worshippers will worship the Father in spirit and in truth, for the Father is seeking such to worship Him.'

The astonishing truth was that Almighty God was searching for the worship of this rejected woman who herself had been searching for love for all of her life. The Lord Jesus is the same God today! When the Lord revealed to a Samaritan woman that He was the Messiah that she and her people were looking for, her life was transformed. Instead of creeping back into the city and into isolation, she went back and told the others of the one who had challenged and changed her life by His words. God's word is still transforming lives today. The people of the town of Sychar came to see and hear Jesus for themselves. They discovered that all that this woman had told them was true and many of them came to a personal faith in Christ. The Lord's disciples who were there, were shocked that He spoke to a Samaritan woman and astonished at the outcome, but the Son of God hadn't come to earn respectability, He had come to save sinners. He went on to teach the disciples and said,

'One sows and another reaps.'

Because of these things, the word of God had already been sown in Samaria when Philip was led there by the Spirit. God's purpose was to reap a harvest.

When Philip went into the area and began to preach, as previously with Stephen, miraculous signs of deliverance and healing confirmed the authority of his message. Powerful proclamation of the gospel was made, but there was opposition to it. It came in the guise of counterfeit experience. Simon Magus had been the leader of a cult in the main town. He had practiced magic and made great claims about himself, whereas in reality he was a confidence trickster in spiritual confusion. Even though he was a clever man and had probably read the literature that various philosophers and theologians had left, he was a fool in his understanding.

Justin, one of the post apostolic leaders in the early church had come from Samaria himself. He wrote about Simon and said that he had come from a village called Gitta and that his partner Helen was a former prostitute. Simon had supposedly delivered her from possessing a variety of female bodies, in order to become a goddess in partnership with himself. He claimed personal divinity. The message he gave to the people was of salvation by faith in him and Helen, with no requirement to stop sinning. This kind of a message appealed to people who wanted a spiritual experience that allowed them to indulge their sinful appetites. Irenaeus, another post apostolic leader in the early church said that Simon Magus was the first major heretic. He was a dangerous man at that time and there have been dangerous people who have deviated from the truth of salvation through faith in Christ alone all through history!

When Simon heard Philip preach, he was amazed at the miracles which followed and he wanted to know how they were done. He believed Philip's message about Jesus and was baptized along with many others. The apostles who had been able to remain in Jerusalem heard what was happening in Samaria and Peter and John came down to see all that was happening for themselves.

When they met these new Christians, they laid hands on them and prayed that they might receive the Holy Spirit. God answered prayer and gave the evidence of His power in them. When Simon saw this, he wanted to be able to lay hands on people himself, so that they could receive spiritual power. However his motives were egotistical and not to honour Christ and he offered Peter and John money to enable him to do this. He wanted power for himself so he could peddle bogus spiritual experiences to the people around him. It still happens! Even though this practice has come in many varied disguises, the devious association between money, power and spiritual experience has never gone away.

Peter turned to Simon and said in clear and strong rebuke,

'Your money perish with you, because you thought that the gift of God could be purchased with money! You have neither part nor portion in this matter, for your heart is not right in the sight of God.'

Simon was concerned that neither he nor his money perish and he asked the apostles to pray that none of the things they had said would happen.

Initially he had sounded genuine, he had looked the part, but he was motivated by a spirit other than the Holy Spirit. His counterfeit experience was challenged by Peter and his influence on the new believers stopped, but according to the records of early church historians, it didn't appear as if even this repentance was genuine. Spiritual discernment always has been a necessary part of church growth.

Philip had been used to see revival break out in Samaria. The apostles were ministering there, crowds were coming to faith in Christ, miracles were happening, but Philip was called to leave it all and go south to the desert road which led to Gaza. God's purposes were ongoing, Jesus was at the centre of them and Philip was called to be further involved in them. When he came to the desert road, an Ethiopian eunuch was travelling south in his chariot. In those days, Ethiopia was a sizable kingdom to the south of Egypt. This eunuch was in charge of all of the wealth of the Candice, or queen of the country. He was a man with considerable responsibility, like a present day chancellor of the exchequer in the UK. As a eunuch, he would not have been allowed into the temple at Jerusalem, nor have been accepted fully as a proselyte to Judaism, but he was seeking the truth of God in the scriptures.

The Spirit of God spoke to Philip and told him to catch up with the chariot and speak to this searching man who was in it. What a privilege to be God's messenger! His word is still bringing a message to people who are searching for the value and purpose of their life.

As Philip drew alongside the chariot, he heard the eunuch reading from the prophet Isaiah,

'He was led as a lamb to the slaughter and as sheep before its shearers is silent, so he didn't open His mouth. In His humiliation, His justice was taken away. Who will declare His generation, for His life is taken from the earth.'

When Philip asked him if he understood what he was reading, he answered,

'How can I unless someone guides me?'

Then he invited Philip to climb up into the chariot and help him to understand who the prophet Isaiah was referring to.

The sacrificial system that offered a lamb to die in the place of men had been instituted in the days of Moses. Then, the Angel of Death had passed over the houses of the children of Israel in Egypt because they had obediently painted the lintels of the doorway of their homes with blood from a year old perfect lamb. Their Egyptian captors had lost the firstborn son of every household when this messenger of death had moved through the land that night and there was no blood over the doorways of their homes. Because of their deliverance, when the Angel of death had passed over their houses, the children of Israel called it the 'Passover night.' Following their emancipation from slavery in Egypt they had offered a perfect lamb as a burnt offering to God every year in thanksgiving for their deliverance and to make atonement for their sin. These sacrifices were at the very heart of the Jewish religion. When Jesus began His earthly ministry at the river Jordan, John the Baptist pointed to Him and declared to all the people there,

'Behold the lamb of God who takes away the sin of the world!'

Jesus was and is God's sacrificial lamb and as Philip and the Ethiopian considered Isaiah's prophesy, understanding came to the eunuch's heart. He immediately responded by requesting to be baptized as a believer in Jesus Christ, the Son of God. Baptism as a Christian was a significant action to take. It symbolised identifying with Jesus as the divine Saviour. For the Jews it meant being prepared to be rejected by their families. In the Roman empire it meant identifying with the one who said that He was the way, the truth, the life and the only way to God and refusing all other demands for worship. When Caesar demanded worship as a deity, this could have brought the death penalty to those who would not bow before him. Many did lay down their life in the coliseum in Rome, rather than deny Christ as their Saviour.

The Ethiopian eunuch had said, 'Here is water; what hinders me from being baptized?' and Philip had replied, 'If you believe with all your heart, you may.'

He did and they stopped the chariot and went down to the water. As they stepped into it, the Eunuch was declaring his full identity as a believer in a full salvation through the blood of Jesus Christ, the lamb of God. As Philip lowered his body under the water, the Eunuch's action was saying, 'I am buried with the Christ who died for me.'

When Philip lifted him out of the water he was symbolically saying,

'I live in Christ, because Jesus lives in me in the person and by the power of His Holy Spirit.'

His baptism was a testimony of this new personal faith, to Philip, a member of the Christian church, before the world, before the demons of hell and to the God of heaven.

As soon as the ceremony was complete, the Spirit of God caught Philip away to Azotus, a Philistine city about twenty miles north of Gaza. However, the Eunuch was not on his own, because the Spirit of God was in his life and Christ was with him!

The obedience of this deacon who had responded to God's call to leave a revival in order to reach one man, resulted in the gospel being taken into Africa. The church was growing!

Chapter 6
Saul's Conversion

Saul of Tarsus, who had been at the scene of Stephen's death, was still breathing out murderous threats against the disciples. As a well educated Pharisee, who had kept the laws of his religion, he was full of self-righteous anger against any sect that would dare to challenge what he considered to be authentic Judaism.

Shortly before His death, Jesus had said to His disciples,

'I am the way, the truth and the life, no one comes to the Father except through me.'

He had declared that He was the only way into the very presence of God. Now after His death and resurrection, the disciples were called, 'Followers of the Way.'

After Pentecost the gospel had spread far and wide and many people were coming to God through faith in Christ.

Saul was furious and determined to stop what he considered to be a dangerous heresy, even if he had to kill its participants.

It is an amazing fact that religion can blind the eyes of people to God's plan of salvation.

Saul went to the high priest and asked him for letters of authority to go to the synagogue in the Syrian town of Damascus and eradicate any of Followers of the Way that he found there. He was given approval to bring them back in chains to Jerusalem. The burning resentment in his heart blinded him to the realization that he was no more than an angry sinner setting himself against the purposes of a holy God. As he drew near to the city, a light of spectacular intensity focused on him. Under its heavenly brilliance he crashed to the ground and lay prostrate, unable to move. His arrogance was completely humbled as he heard a voice personally challenging him.

'Saul, Saul, why are you persecuting me?'

'Who are you, Lord?'

He knew that whoever was speaking to him had divine authority. He was Lord. Completely at the end of his natural resources he listened to Almighty God speaking to him.

'I am Jesus, whom you are persecuting. It is hard for you to kick against the goads.'

The goad were pointed sticks that were used for prodding cattle to make them move.

Trembling in shock and humiliation he answered,

'Lord what do you want me to do?'

The spoken Word of God had revealed Jesus to him and at last he was willing to listen and obey. This brilliant student of philosophy, politics and law, realized that the voice he had heard was far greater than one of a mere academic record. Many people are still only willing to acknowledge God speaking to them when they are brought completely to an end of their own natural resources. God in His mercy can heal and restore, but if people would come willingly before the sin of rebellion against God had damaged their lives, how much happier they would be. Nevertheless Jesus once said that those who were forgiven for a lot of sin, would in return be filled with a lot of love for God.

Flashbacks to the scene of Stephen's martyrdom and the words of other disciples whom he had persecuted, would have found a fresh significance in Saul's mind.

This God who had humbled and challenged him, gave him direction.

'Arise, go into the city and you will be told what you must do.'

Saul had been more used to telling other people what to do than being told himself, but now he had no alternative than to listen to instruction. The people who had been on the journey to Damascus with him were in total confusion. They had heard a voice but not understood it and seen a bright light but not been able to realize who was speaking. Falteringly Saul stood up and opened his eyes, only to discover that he was totally blind.

This revelation was not only of a physical disability, but of a spiritual reality.

Before people can walk in God's way, they need to be made aware of their own spiritual blindness!

Devastated, Saul was taken by the hand and led into the city, where he didn't eat or drink anything for three days. It was almost as if God had taken him on his own Christ like experience of death before being buried in the tomb for that same period of time.

In Damascus there was a disciple called Ananias. Unlike his earlier namesake, this man was utterly real with the Lord. He was a man of prayer and God gave him revelation. In a vision he was given the instruction to go the house of Judas, in Straight Street and ask for Saul of Tarsus. This man Judas was totally unlike his earlier namesake. He was willing to open his home even in the face of impending danger.

The vision and instructions that Ananias had been given, were totally specific. There was nothing vague or mystical about them. He knew exactly what he was called to do, but even though he was a Godly man of faith, he was fearful! He knew that Saul had done a lot of damage to the Christians in Jerusalem and that he had come to Damascus on an officially validated program of religious persecution.- He was there to arrest the believers.

Ananias knew all of these things, but when God said 'Go!' he went!

It had been revealed to him that Saul, this desperate opponent of the gospel, was going to be a missionary for Jesus, who would be prepared to go through persecution himself, in order to be a witness for his Saviour.

What a revelation Ananias had been given! He immediately went to Judas's house and on entering said,

'Brother Saul, the Lord Jesus, who appeared to you on the road as you came, has sent me that you may receive your sight and be filled with the Holy Spirit!'

As these powerful words God had spoken through this simple disciple entered Saul's mind, the reality of what God had done reverberated through his life. Ananias was not heard of again in scripture, but his obedient service here was of eternal significance.

Saul had become a spiritual brother with this believer! Immediately his eyes opened and he was given fresh vision, both physically and spiritually. He rose to his feet and was baptised. He ate and was strengthened. He went and spent some days with the believers in Damascus that he had come to imprison and confessed that Jesus was his Lord too! It was like a resurrection! Saul of Tarsus was a new man, belonging to Jesus Christ!

With this fresh revelation burning in his soul, he went to the synagogue, strengthened to meet with the very people who had been waiting for him to come and imprison the believers. A clarity of conviction made his message all the more shocking to the congregation who gathered there.

'This Christ is the Son of God!'

Daily as he gained fresh strength, he declared his personal testimony to all the Jews who lived in Damascus. They were flabbergasted. Soon some of them hatched a plan to murder this man who they felt had betrayed them. He was facing the very attitudes and threats that he himself had made against the believers he had come to arrest. A number of the Jews kept the city gate under observation twenty four hours a day so that they could kill him when he left at its one point of entry and exit. The disciples of Christ, who must at first have received him with a great deal of caution, now were concerned for his preservation. They put him into a large woven basket that was strong enough to carry bales of hay or wool, then bound it round with ropes and lowered it over the city walls.

The antagonist of the gospel who had approached Damascus in religious pride and personal wrath, armed with the authority to arrest believers, was helped by them to escape with his life. He had come with hatred and left with a testimony of divine grace to share with those in the faith in Jerusalem. However, his conversion didn't remove all of his problems. In fact it gave him more!

When he arrived in Jerusalem the Christians there did not believe he was genuine. They remembered the man with blood on his hands going on a mission to imprison their brothers in Christ and they were afraid of him.

Previously he had been held in esteem by the Sanhedrin and given respect by the Jewish groups like the Hellenists who had opposed Stephen. Paul now faced suspicion and rejection from all sides, but God knew his heart.

Barnabas, the Cypriot 'son of encouragement' who had joined with Peter and the other apostles in their earlier powerful testimony in Jerusalem, now identified with Saul. He brought him to the apostles and told them how this former antagonist had met the Lord on the Damascus road and become an ambassador for Christ. When he shared what Saul had done first in the Syrian capital and how he had wanted to join the church in Jerusalem, the apostles received him. As a result, he travelled around the whole local area and made a bold confession of his faith in Christ. With his previous training and present experience, he had a God given ability to demonstrate from scripture the truth of his new faith. The Hellenist group were so angry that they attempted to murder him while he was in the city. The Lord had previously told Ananias that Saul would be shown how many things he would suffer for the gospel. People had already tried to kill him on two occasions and he had only been a believer for a brief time.

The Christian way was no easy path of escape for Saul of Tarsus. God did not say it would be for any true believer throughout history. Jesus had previously said to His disciples, that if anyone wanted to come with Him, they must take up their cross and follow Him. However the Lord again made a way of escape for this new convert who was going to become a powerful witness throughout the Roman Empire. The believers in Jerusalem brought him to Caesarea, a port on the Mediterranean sea. From there he was sent to Tarsus where as well as being a witness of his faith throughout the area, he must have studied the scriptures and quietly learnt from the Lord for several years. God had saved this man for a ministry that would be of world changing significance. This period of grounding in the truths of Christ and of growth in Christian character were an essential part of the Lord's plan for Saul. We all need this grounding.

During this period a time of real blessing and further expansion came to the churches in Judea, Galilee and Samaria, as the Holy Spirit moved through the lives of their individual members. The purpose of Almighty God was to build His church in the name of His Son and save sinners from going to a lost eternity. This purpose was not only being outworked in the local assemblies near Jerusalem but in the heart and life of Saul of Tarsus. The same purpose of God's saving grace is still at work in the lives of all who will respond to His word!

Chapter 7
Peter's Position

Caesarea of Philippi, a place of outstanding natural beauty near the foot of Mount Hermon, nestled beside one of the main sources of the river Jordan. Decisive battles had been fought there, pagan shrines had been erected there, Herod the Great had built a marble temple there to honour Augustus Caesar and Jesus of Nazareth had stood there and asked His followers,

'Who do men say that I, the Son of Man, am?'

The significance of the place was far outweighed by Simon Peter's reply.

'You are the Christ, the anointed, the Son of the living God!'

Jesus answered him not only with a blessing, but with a commission.

'Blessed are you Simon Bar-Jonah, for flesh and blood has not revealed this to you but my Father who is in heaven. And I say unto you that you are Peter and on this rock I will build my church.'

The name Petros meant a small rock. Later he wrote a letter to Christian believers who were being hounded to martyrdom by the emperor Nero and spoke to them of a faith more precious than gold tested by fire. He spoke to them of,

'Coming to Him as to a living stone rejected indeed my men but chosen by God and precious.'

Speaking of Jesus, he quoted the prophet Isaiah,

'Behold I lay in Zion. A chief cornerstone, elect precious, And he who believes on Him will by no means be put to shame.'

The Roman emperor Nero eventually committed suicide when his own people turned against him following the over thirty years of diabolical havoc that he had caused.

In the midst of all of this Peter had written to these believers who would rather have laid down their own lives than deny Christ and said,

'You also as living stones are being built up a spiritual house, a holy priesthood, to offer spiritual sacrifices acceptable to God through Jesus Christ.'

Like Peter, these believers were being called to be living stones built on the foundation rock of Christ Himself.

Shortly after Peter had made his initial confession of the identity of Jesus, the Lord began to reveal that His purpose was to go to Jerusalem to be accused, killed and raised again on the third day. Peter could neither accept this nor understand it:

'Far be it Lord. This won't happen to you.'

Jesus rebuked him for not understanding what he was saying. Peter's words were inspired by Satan's desire to avoid the consequences of the work of the cross of Calvary.

Later in the upper room before Christ's final Passover supper, this brash disciple again spoke out,

'Lord, I am ready to go with you, both to prison and to death.'

The Jewish day was counted from sunset to sunset and it was evening when he said this.

Christ's answer came, warning him of his impending denial before even the next dawn broke.

'The rooster shall not crow this day before you will deny three times that you know me.'

That night, Jesus was arrested in the garden of Gethsemane and taken to the high priest's house for an illegal trial. On three separate occasions people identified Peter with the Galilean Jesus.

In fear, he denied it twice and the third time he ended up swearing about it.

On his way from the trial when Jesus simply looked at Peter, he fled from the house. He remembered that his master had warned him of this and he ran out into the night, a weeping, broken man.

After Calvary, when news came of the resurrection, Peter considered all that he had heard and seen, but still did not come to believing faith. Days later when he had gone back to his boat to fish, the other disciples went with him, but their efforts were fruitless. When they returned to the shore, Jesus was at the lakeside calling to them.

'Have you any food? — Cast your nets on the other side of the boat and you will!'

Obedience to this simple instruction brought a catch that was too heavy to haul over the side of their vessel. In shock they recognised their risen Lord and responded to His invitation to come to Him. They dragged the nets towards the shore, where He had made a fire. He told them to bring some fish to roast and eat and then addressed Peter directly.

'Simon, son of Jonah, do you love me more than these?'

Christ used the word meaning divine love and used it again when He asked the question a second time.

The third time He asked the question, He used another word, meaning brotherly love.

'Simon son of Jonah; Do you love me!?'

This man who had previously relied on human strength and failed miserably, knew that he needed Christ's forgiveness. He needed God's mercy and he needed divine power. The challenge of Christ's word to Peter applies personally to each one of our hearts!

The desperate fisherman cried out in repentant faith,

'Lord you know all things. You know that I love you!'

His threefold denial was brought to a threefold confession of faith. Then this was followed by a threefold commissioning to service.

'Feed my sheep! Tend my lambs! Feed my sheep!'

He was warned that he couldn't do this in his own natural strength and that his life would not be in his own hands.

Pentecost had come and Peter who had known forgiveness because of Calvary, was serving the good Shepherd by caring for the flock of new believers.

He knew that he was a sinner saved by grace and strengthened by the power of the Holy Spirit. As he travelled around the country following Stephen's martyrdom and Saul's conversion, he wanted everyone else to come to a place of personal salvation in Christ as well.

50

One day he went to the little town of Lydda, to meet with some people who had set themselves apart in Christ's name, to worship God. Lydda was about twenty five miles from Jerusalem, on a busy trade route. Of the people who had gathered with the Christians there, one was a paralyzed man called Aeneas. He had been crippled for eight years. In Pentecostal power, with a command that sounded like an echo of the words Jesus had spoken during His earthly ministry to the cripple who had been lowered through the roof, Peter spoke to Aeneas,

'Jesus the Christ heals you. Arise and make your bed!'

His command wasn't given in his own name, or because of his own strength or willpower. He was moving in the power and will of God!

Aeneas's days as a helpless cripple were finished as Peter spoke. At that moment he arose as living evidence that God was at work. As a result, everybody who knew him in and around the area came to faith in Jesus because the same Holy Spirit who was working through Peter, worked in their lives too! God was building His church and He used Peter in a healing ministry and Aeneas as a witness of divine involvement with needy lives.

Ten miles beyond Lydda, in Joppa, the present day port of Tel Aviv, another little group of believers met to share in this fellowship of faith. Among them was a woman whose name Tabitha in Aramaic and Dorcas in Greek, both meant gazelle. She had been a spiritual sister in Christ whose service and kindness were widely known and respected, but she had died. The disciples in Joppa had laid out her body in an upstairs room, in preparation for her burial. The more normal practise of having a prompt funeral was delayed so that her grieving friends could send a message to Peter in Lydda, asking him to come quickly to see this woman who had been such a blessing to them all.

When he arrived, in tears they showed him the garments she had made for them. He must have remembered the similar situation the Lord faced when He had been called to Jairus's dead daughter. Not only in healing, but in all of his Christian life, Peter now sought to follow the example that Jesus had shown.

He sent all of the people from the room where Tabitha was laying and spoke to her corpse in God-given-faith.

'Tabitha, arise!'

She opened her eyes and taking Peter's hand, stood to her feet. She was alive! The power of God was there! The moving of the Holy Spirit through Peter and the other disciples was not resuscitating Judaism, or exhibiting sensationalism. It was a living demonstration of new spiritual life that had a practical outworking. As the news of this latest miracle spread, it was an effective means of calling many people in the area to faith in Christ.

Peter stayed for some time in Joppa with a man called Simon who worked as a tanner. His job involved skinning the dead animals and leaving the hide to dry in the heat. The odour at times would have been profound and the task would have been offensive to practising Jews. Peter had taken another step of faith when he stayed with him for the sake of the gospel. Even though he didn't fully understand, the Lord was leading him into a further realm of Christian service.

Caesarea was another Mediterranean port further to the north. A Roman centurion called Cornelius was stationed there as a member of the Italian regiment. His father had been a slave who had been emancipated. Cornelius had worked his way up through the ranks of the Roman army to become a non commissioned officer. He was a soldier and had seen people dying on the battlefield, but yet he had a deep longing in his heart to know the living God. He was a sincere man of prayer and the God whom he was seeking answered him. In a vision he saw and heard an angelic visitor tell him to send a message to Joppa and ask for Simon Peter, who was lodging with Simon the tanner in his house by the sea. When he got there he would be instructed in what to do next. The command was specific and Cornelius recognised its source. Like the centurion that Jesus had spoken to in His ministry in Capernaum, he knew the authority of God's word.

This monotheistic, God fearing Gentile was being divinely prepared to hear of the way of salvation and the apostle Peter was being prepared to bring the gospel of Christ to him. At midday, in the heat of the sun, while Peter was praying on the flat roof of Simon's house overlooking the sea, he fell into a kind of trance and saw a sheet holding all kinds of creatures that were unclean under the Jewish law. It was being lowered down from heaven. He heard a command telling him to kill and eat one of the animals but he refused to do it. Even though he was not rigid in his religious practises, he had never eaten anything that was common and unclean and he wasn't going to start: But the Lord spoke to him again,

'What God has cleansed, you must not call common.'

He woke up and while he was still wondering what on earth the strange vision meant, the Holy Spirit spoke to him and said,

'Behold, three men are seeking you. Arise therefore, go down and go with them, doubting nothing; for I have sent them!'

This happened just before the messengers from Cornelius called at Simon's door and asked for him.

With such an assurance from the Lord, Peter went to Caesarea the next day. There Cornelius was waiting for him in almost superstitious awe, but Peter would have none of it. After explaining how the Lord had told him to go and mix with this Gentile company, the meaning of his earlier vision became clear. His original commission really had meant 'go into all the world and preach the gospel.' God didn't have favourites. The gospel of Christ was for absolutely everyone who would turn to Him for forgiveness and salvation.

Peter explained how God had anointed Jesus with the Spirit and then sent Him with power to heal and cast out demons. He told how the apostles had been witnesses of what Christ had done and of how He had been crucified in Jerusalem. God had raised Him up on the third day and ordained Him to be the final judge of the living and of the dead. In His name there was forgiveness for sin. As Peter was still speaking, the Holy Spirit came down upon the people who had gathered in Caesarea with the same display of power that He had manifested on the day of Pentecost. The crowd began to speak in other tongues and worship the Lord. It was a fresh revelation of the purpose of God. They knew they were saved, redeemed, forgiven and given a place in God's family. Their lives had been transformed not by Peter's eloquence or Cornelius's goodness, but by God's grace and the power of the Holy Spirit. In obedience to Peter's directing and as a public testimony of their faith in Christ, they were all baptized in water. God's plan of salvation that had cleansed the sinner, healed the sick, raised the dead was now for anyone in the world who would surrender their life to the Saviour. The impact of all that had happened in the home of Cornelius not only reverberated throughout Caesarea and Jerusalem but throughout heaven itself!

When the other apostles heard that the Gentiles had received the word of God, Peter went to them and gave a clear report of what had happened. The initial opposition from the traditional Jewish element was overwhelmed by the praise of God's people as they understood the revelation that the people had received in the house of Cornelius.

'In truth I perceive that God shows no partiality—— He is Lord of all!'

They recognised that now Cornelius had given his life to Jesus, there were Gentiles among the believers too. They had a fresh understanding that the Spirit of Christ was not only bringing Jewish people into a relationship with the living God, but people from other nations were being saved through faith in Him as well. The promise of His power, the purity of His salvation and the purpose of His life, were being demonstrated in all those who the Lord was calling.

However when God moves in peoples lives, the devil often comes to try and spoil their response. Sometimes it may be through temptation, sometimes through subtle distraction and sometimes through outright opposition. True revival has often seemed to go hand in hand with persecution. Vast numbers in a congregation are not necessarily the evidence of God's blessing. Sometimes church growth has been inspired by political motivation, or financial gain. Sometimes, especially recently in the Western culture, public entertainment and psychological manipulation have drawn appreciative audiences. None of these things will survive the purifying fires that will face every true believer. Satan's attacks on God's work can be so challenging that earthly life can literally be at stake. Throughout history many Christians have been called to martyrdom for their faith. Some religions promote martyrdom so that others will die. Christ had set the pattern of laying His own life down, so that others could live

King Herod Agrippa was the grandson of Herod the Great, the despot who had given the orders to kill all the male children in Bethlehem following Christ's birth. Agrippa was not any better than his grandfather and had lead an argumentative, immoral, financially corrupt life. He reigned from thirty seven to forty four A.D. Under Roman authority he had been set up as the puppet king of Judea and Samaria and had kept his position through fear and intrigue. Mixing religion and politics together entirely for his own ends, he was violently opposed to the Christian faith. He had James the brother of John killed by the sword. The hard line Jews who had heard of the mixed-race Samaritans and then of the Gentile Cornelius becoming disciples of Christ, were pleased by this. As a result Agrippa went on to arrest Peter. During the time that the Jews were celebrating the Passover feast, he threw the apostle Peter into prison and placed him on 'death row' under strict guard. Two soldiers were stationed outside his prison door along with two others, one chained to each arm. Peter's ministry of being used to build the church of Christ, was not always conducive to his natural comfort! However he found his rest through faith in God.

Freedom is a precious privilege. That night in the prison cell, between his guards, Peter was sleeping! Agrippa was still hating and scheming from his puppet throne. It really is interesting to think who really was imprisoned and who was at liberty. Peter possessed a faith that set him free to follow Jesus. Nevertheless, when an angel of the Lord came to where he was, he just didn't understand what was happening. The angel struck him on the side, a bright light filled the prison cell and he heard a voice speaking,

'Arise quickly; Gird yourself and tie on your sandals! —- Put on your garment and follow me!'

The chains fell from his wrists and he followed the angel past the inner guards and then the outer guard posts, through the iron prison gates and out into the city.

When he looked around the angel of the Lord had gone. The angel's work was done, but Peter had more to do while serving God on earth!

As he stood in the darkness, on the streets of Jerusalem, it took him a while to realize what had actually happened. He had escaped from death row and he was a free man.

Knowing that the other believers would be praying for him he went straight to the house of John Mark's mother, where they would be meeting together. Arriving there he knocked on the door and a girl called Rhoda came to open it.

'Who is there?'

When Peter answered, she didn't open the door, but ran back into the room where the others were praying for his release.

'It's Peter! He is at the door!'

'Don't be silly! He's in prison.'

She must be really out of order. Didn't she realize how important it was to pray for his release?!

Peter kept knocking!

Eventually when she insisted that he really was at the door, they let him in.

During His earthly ministry, Jesus had said,

'If you have faith as grain of mustard seed, you will say to this mountain, 'Move from here to there,' and it will move!'

At least these disciples in Mary's house had the faith to ask! Maybe they had thought there was a possibility that Peter could have been discharged through the legal process on the next day, but that would have been unlikely. Instead, God had answered their prayers in a way that was more dramatic than they had imagined or expected. It is God's prerogative as to how He answers prayer! Peter had almost found it easier to get out of prison than into the prayer meeting!

Where the Spirit of the Lord is there is liberty. Peter had known the freedom of peace with God, even in the prison cell. He had found that literal freedom had come as he had obeyed the message that he had been given by the angel of the Lord. When he stood outside the prison gates in the city of Jerusalem, he knew that it was all completely God's work and not his own. He went to tell James, the Lord's brother what had happened. After the resurrection of Jesus, James had come to personal faith himself and was leading the Jerusalem church. Peter had seen that the power of God could open doors supernaturally, or use the hands of a servant girl in His purposes. The prayers of the group in the home of Mary, the mother of John Mark, had been answered. Even though they had needed to learn to respond more readily in faith to what God was doing, the Lord had used them in a way that Satan had not been able to defeat.

When day broke and Herod Agrippa found that his prize prisoner had gone, he was livid. He searched for Peter everywhere. Unable to find him, he had the prison guards executed. He went down to Caesarea and then his anger was inflamed against the residents of Tyre and Sidon. Maybe he thought Peter had escaped from one of these ports in a ship.

In order to gain his goodwill and material provisions, the citizens of Tyre and Sidon blasphemously appealed to his pride. Herod sat on a throne, dressed in royal apparel and as they listened to him making a speech, they began to shout in unison,

'The voice of a god and not of a man!'

Satan had given his values to Agrippa but this time he had gone too far. Under divine judgement he collapsed from his throne and died in agony before the eyes of the very people who had appealed to his self indulgent vanity.

Despite all of the opposition, the number of the believers that he had persecuted continued to grow and declare the word of the Lord. God was building His church!

He still is!

Chapter 8
Church Growth God's Way

Persecution following Stephen's death had scattered the believers far and wide, but by the power of the Holy Spirit, wherever they went they preached the gospel! It wasn't a masochistic message of defeated escapism, it was a glorious declaration of eternal salvation! The fruit of their message brought increase, encouragement, identity and expression to the church. The word of God that flowed from their hearts and from their lips, was powerful, but as yet these believers had still not publically preached to any Gentiles. They had initially spoken only to the diaspora of Israel who had been scattered around the Roman empire. Then some of the Hellenist Jews who had been converted following Stephen's martyrdom, came to Antioch and preached to the Greek people there. As a result, many of them became committed followers of 'The Way.'

When Jesus had given His original commission to the disciples, He had told them,

'I send the promise of my Father upon you, but tarry in the city of Jerusalem until you are endued with power from on high.'

Christ had kept His word and they had been baptized in the Holy Spirit. His instructions had been to take the gospel to Jerusalem, then Judea and Samaria and finally into all the world. Their initial reticence to do this had been changed by the circumstances that had unfolded. Firstly some of the mixed race Samaritans had become believers, then Cornelius the Gentile had been converted and now the gospel was being preached in Antioch (two hundred miles north of Tyre and Sidon.)

Antioch, the capital of Syria was the third largest city in the Roman empire. It was a cosmopolitan mixture of about half a million people, from Hebrew, Roman and Arab backgrounds. The religious culture of the city was basically pagan and immoral. Situated on the river Orontes, it was about twenty miles inland from the Mediterranean sea. Jerusalem was three hundred miles away, but when the apostles who were there heard of the great response to the gospel in Antioch, they sent Barnabas to find out exactly what was going on. Barnabas had gained an excellent reputation in the Jerusalem church as a discerning and honourable man, full of the Holy Spirit and faith. He was trusted to make a wise assessment of the situation and when he arrived and saw that what had happened was a genuine turning to Christ; he was overjoyed. This was no gimmick, it was God's work. People had recognised who Jesus was and responded to the gospel call to leave their old way of life. They had come into the new and Godly way of living that had been unveiled at the cross of Calvary.

Barnabas, the 'son of encouragement' had a ministry to these new believers. He encouraged them to follow the Lord with all their heart and as a result even more were added to the church. Encouragement is a precious ministry. When Barnabas had seen what God had done in Antioch, he committed himself to supporting it. The encouragement he brought wasn't just one of back patting and nice smiles; It was one of sacrificial service! He set off to find Saul, who had remained in Tarsus, following the threats on his life in Jerusalem. Barnabas took encouragement to him as well as the people in Antioch! He knew that the man he had introduced to Peter some three years previously had a knowledge of scripture and a gift of teaching which would be invaluable to the new believers there. With this in mind he went and found this converted Pharisee and brought him back to help the new Gentile believers in Jesus, the Jewish Messiah, who had come to bring a message of salvation for all who would believe His word.

Saul may well have remembered the prophesy that Ananias had been given about him when he was in Damascus:

' A chosen vessel to bear my name before the Gentiles, kings and the Children of Israel.'

His renewed ministry wasn't to be in the place he would formerly have chosen, but it was in the place of divine appointment.

God had been faithful to His word. He still is! There is no greater encouragement than that!

In Antioch, the believers not only increased in number and were encouraged, but they were given a new identity. This was the first time they had been called 'Christians.' The people observed that they didn't keep rigidly to the Jewish rituals and they were not pagans, or into Greek mythology, so they called them 'Christ's ones.' At first it was almost a derogatory term, but later the name 'Christian' identified the followers of Jesus from every nation. It signified their identification with the Christ, who had come into the world to save men and women who were spiritually perishing. Identification wasn't simply in being called by Christ's name, it was demonstrated by the changed conduct in the lives of His followers.

Agabus, a prophet from the Jerusalem church came down to be with the new Christians in Antioch. He warned the people there of a world famine that was going to come to Jerusalem. Josephus and Suetonius, Roman historians both recorded a great famine that struck Israel and the surrounding nations during the year 45-46 AD and Josephus referred to famine relief that came from around the Antioch area. The new converts had contributed from their own possessions to support the church in Jerusalem because of a God given desire to help their fellow believers. This expression of Christian love and care accompanied their verbal confession of faith.

Saul had been called in to help in Antioch and already this new church was sending out help to others. He and Barnabas took this aid and gave it to the leaders of the Jerusalem church. These were men who had taught and adhered to the scriptures, in order to care for the spiritual needs of the growing congregation. It was in Jerusalem that church leaders were firstly called 'elders' and given responsibility for the spiritual oversight of the congregation. They themselves were called to lead exemplary lives and give clear biblical instruction. The deacons who had been appointed earlier, were also spiritual men who had been charged with the responsibility of caring for various practical needs within the church.

Stephen's life was still bearing fruit after his death. Saul of Tarsus, who had held the jackets of those who stoned Stephen, was now himself a Christian missionary. Soon his very name would be translated from the Hebrew 'Saul,' to the Roman 'Paul,' commissioned to be the apostle to the Gentiles!

God's ways are amazing - He even brings blessing out of cursing!

Growth and life in the church had become the God-given purpose of Paul's own life.

In Antioch, this multicultural gathering of the early Christians, was the missionary church from which the apostle would launch out with the gospel across the Roman empire. The indwelling Holy Spirit had given this former persecutor the desire to take the message of salvation through faith in Christ alone into all the world.

The same Saviour who had called the first disciples from their fishing boats at the side of Galilee, was now inspiring a group of Gentile believers to have a part in declaring His message to the nations.

In the church in Antioch, as well as men able to teach scriptures, there were those with the gift of prophesy. They had been drawn from different races and backgrounds to one Saviour.

Simeon, called Niger, had probably been a liberated slave. He may even have been the very Simeon who helped to carry the cross of Christ to the hill outside Jerusalem.

Lucius, from the north African town of Cyrene, was a man of faithful prayer who desired to spread the gospel. He himself became a companion of Paul on a later missionary journey.

Manaen was one of Christ's unlikely believers. He was the foster brother of Herod Antipas, who the Lord Jesus had called, 'That fox!' Herod Agrippa was his nephew. Herod Antipas had beheaded John the Baptist, for challenging him about living with his sister-in-law. Manaen's natural family background had not been a pleasant one, but the Lord had called him into God's family. These men had also been given a prophetic gifting and been called to serve the Lord with an anointed ministry at the church. It had a powerful effect. Barnabas and

Paul with Simeon, Lucius and Manaen, fasted and prayed together. As they sought the Lord in this earnest union, prophetic instruction was given to set Paul and Barnabas apart for the further work that God had called them to do. They were to go and take the message of Jesus to the people of Cyprus and beyond.

In obedience to this directing, Simeon, Lucius and Manaen laid hands on Paul and Barnabas and prayed that they would be empowered by God for the task ahead. John Mark, Barnabas' nephew, went with them as an assistant.

Seleucia was the nearest seaport, about five miles north of where the river Orontes flowed into the Mediterranean. They boarded a ship there and sailed to Salamis, the chief commercial centre and sea port in Cyprus. For Barnabas this was home territory, but he went back as a man with a new message. He and Paul entered the Synagogue and proclaimed their faith in Christ, before going on to Paphos, the capital to do the same there. If they had preached to the Gentiles first, the Jews would not have listened to them. Like many of the other cities in the Roman empire, Paphos was a hotbed of immorality. It was there that the seat of Roman government was established, but so also was the worship of Venus. When they began to preach the gospel, it was a renegade Jew who was their immediate source of opposition. He was a sorcerer called Elymas, Son of Jesus. He had a religious background and the right name, but he was certainly not born again by the Holy Spirit. He was not a true son of God, but a false prophet, full of deceit and fraud.

The Roman proconsul for the island was an intelligent man called Sergius Paulus and Bar Jesus was with him. When Sergius Paulus knew that Paul and Barnabas were in the vicinity, he wanted to hear what they had to say, but Bar-Jesus argued against their message. Paul turned and with Spirit-filled authority rebuked him.

This man was not a 'son of Jesus,' he was a son of the devil who perverted the truth for his own unrighteous purposes. Because he wilfully stood in the way of a genuine enquirer into Christian truth, Paul declared God's judgement upon him.

'The hand of the Lord is upon you and you shall be blind, not seeing the sun for a time.'

Perhaps Paul remembered his own spiritual and physical blindness before he was converted.

Elymas was suddenly struggling in a dark mist, asking someone to take him by the hand to show him the way.

Sergius Paulus was astonished to see what had happened and immediately believed the truth of the message that Paul and Barnabas had brought to him. On this very first over sea's missionary journey they encountered opposition from the devil that God turned into an opportunity for His glory. Satan seeks to hinder the clear message of Christ from being proclaimed, but the gospel in the power of the Holy Spirit still brings salvation!

After their time on Cyprus, Paul and Barnabas sailed north across the Mediterranean to the town of Perga, in what is present day Turkey. No sooner had they arrived, than John Mark left them and went back to Jerusalem. True Christian ministry involves spiritual conflict and perhaps the still youthful John Mark found the stress and pressure more than he had anticipated. His desertion did not hinder the mission, but it did cause trouble later between his uncle Barnabas and the apostle Paul. They moved on to the town of Antioch of Pisidia. This was not the Antioch from which they had initially taken leave, but a town that had been founded in 281BC at a junction of the Roman road going through the mountains.

Paul was asked to preach in the synagogue and his sermon has been recorded. He spoke to religious people about God's heart for restoration. When a healthy person cuts their finger it heals, or if they break a bone it mends. Paul's message showed that God's desire was that His people would be restored into a true relationship with Himself. He reminded the congregation in the synagogue that the history of Israel showed how the Lord had brought them out of captivity after four hundred years of slavery in Egypt.

After they entered the Promised land He had destroyed seven national enemies who fought against them. Once they had settled there, for four hundred and fifty years they had been ruled by various Judges in a theocracy, but they had behaved with individualistic selfishness and been dissatisfied with their lot. They wanted to be like the nations around them and rather than having God's sovereign rule, be lead by a human king. God allowed them to have Saul, the son of Kish to be their leader. He stood head and shoulders above his compatriots and in the people's eyes, he appeared to be a splendid man, fit for the task. The people looked at his appearance, but the Lord looked right into his heart and saw his true motives and intentions. Saul failed God and he failed to lead the Children of Israel aright.

Many centuries later, Saul of Tarsus, now the apostle Paul, had been called after Israel's first king. After King Saul's death God gave the people David to be their king. David had been the shepherd boy that Samuel the prophet had anointed in Bethlehem. Despite his many backslidings into desperate sin, God called him 'A man after my own heart.' He had come in sincere repentance and asked the Lord to change his own life around. Many centuries later, Saul of Tarsus had to find the One born in the line of King David as his personal Saviour. Sin always has its consequences. Someone has to pay the price for forgiveness and restoration. The Lord Jesus Christ, the babe of Bethlehem who was born more than eleven hundred years after David, was ready even before earth was created to come and be the Saviour of sinners! His sacrifice on Calvary has an eternal value, for all who truly seek God. King David was forgiven because of what Christ later did on Calvary and so was Saul of Tarsus. We can be too!

The apostle Paul showed how biblical prophesy pointed to Jesus as God's great redeemer who would pay the price for the forgiveness of sin. He declared this to the people in the synagogue, telling them how God had brought Jesus from King David's seed as a Saviour for Israel.

He told them of how John the Baptist had acknowledged Jesus, but the leaders of Judaism had not understood the prophesies that pointed to Him and had handed Him over to be killed. The means of His death had been prophetically declared, before even crucifixion was practised. His burial in a tomb, had been foretold centuries before. In

Christ's day, the practise was to put the of victims of crucifixion in a common grave, but He was indeed buried in a rich man's tomb.

Paul went on to tell the people gathered in that synagogue the greatest evidence of all that Jesus was their promised Messiah.

' God raised Him from the dead!'

Paul's first recorded missionary sermon, was not a message about a dead hero, but of a living Saviour! However, he didn't preach half a gospel, he had told them of God's great work, but he warned them of their need to respond to it and come to Him in personal repentance. To refuse the offer of salvation would be effectively choosing to face the eternal judgement of all who rejected the work of Christ.

After the service outside the synagogue, crowds of gentiles came asking to hear the message of Jesus!

Remembering his own God given commission, Paul quoted from the prophet Isaiah and declared it to all who were there, including the Jews who opposed him.

'I have set you as a light to the Gentiles, that you should be for salvation to the ends of the earth.'

A week later many of the religious Jews and their friends were so furious that they threw Paul and Barnabas out of the city, but God's word had already done it's work. Gentiles had got saved, people had been restored to God and the gospel message had spread all around the region.

However, the message of Christ that was good news for sinners, brought antagonism from the self righteous.

Traditionally Jews had shaken the dust off their feet before re-entering Israel, after they had been in a Gentile country. They did not want to bring pollution into the Promised land. This practise was more sanctimonious than spiritual! After Paul and Barnabas were thrown out of the city, they shook the dust off their own feet to show those Jews who had rejected the message of Christ, that they were no better than infidels. The missionaries had been thrown out, but as they went on to the city of Iconium, the Holy Spirit filled them with joy!

As the Children of Israel had engaged in rebuilding the walls of Jerusalem in the fifth century before Christ, following their release from seventy years captivity in Babylon some hundred years previously, Nehemiah, the prophet of the Old Testament had reminded them that the joy of the Lord was their strength.

As Paul had launched out in missionary service to preach to the Jew first and also to the Gentiles, he was engaged in a work of even greater significance. The joy of the Lord was his strength too as he spent his life in this God-given purpose!

Chapter 9
The Missionary Message

Overseas missionary activity became part of normal Christian practice in the Antioch church. Its members had followed the leading of the Holy Spirit and obeyed God's word by commissioning Paul and Barnabas to go with their blessing and take the Gospel to the people living in Cyprus, Phrygia and Galatia.

When sharing their Christian faith on the island of Cyprus and then on the mainland, Paul and his companion had spoken in the synagogues before addressing Gentile listeners. In the mainland town of Antioch Pisidia, they had headed southeast over the mountains on the Roman road, Via Sebaste, to the city of Iconium. There was a synagogue there and the initial proclamation of the Christian message brought a good response from many of the hearers. However, in previous generations the town had been turned into a Greek city-state and as a result the accompanying philosophies had pervaded its thinking. A myth about creation counterfeited the Genesis record. The Greek gods Prometheus and Athenia, were supposed to have made models of people from the mud left by a devastating flood. After these pagan deities had breathed on the models, they had supposedly come to life.

Paul and Barnabas preached a Christ-centred gospel wherever they went. They boldly spoke of salvation by the grace of God to the people of Iconium and miraculous signs confirmed the truth of their message. However the word of God doesn't always unite everybody. It divides truth from error and as a result, the city of Iconium was divided in its response to what they had heard. Antagonists to the apostolic challenge planned to kill its messengers and so Paul and Barnabas left the place in order to proclaim the message to others. They were willing to die for their testimony but they didn't want to foolishly throw their lives away. Moving on to the town of Lystra, they entered the Roman province of Galatia. While Paul was preaching, a crippled man listened to him and understood that the word he was hearing was true. Paul saw that there was a real response of faith in the man and he knew that God wanted to heal him.

'Stand up straight on your feet!'

Like the cripple Peter and John had spoken to at the gates of the temple in Jerusalem, this man leapt to his feet and walked. The onlookers were astounded. Almighty God had sent supernatural confirmation to Paul's message, but the devil sent superstitious opposition!

The people of Lystra began to shout,

'The gods have come down to us in the likeness of men!'

They thought that Zeus and Hermes had appeared among them!

Fifty years previously a poem had been written as a folk tale recounting how the Greek gods Zeus and Hermes had come to Lystra, looking for food and shelter. Everyone had refused them help except two peasants. In vengeance for the general lack of help they had received, the two gods had drowned everybody there apart from the peasants, before turning their cottage into a golden temple. As a result of this folk story, the inhabitants of the city didn't want to make the same mistake as their forbearers and so they came to worship Paul and Barnabas by sacrificing an oxen to them.

The devil's tactic of appealing to men's ego and materialistic lust has not changed during the centuries!

However, when Paul and Barnabus realized what was going on, they were horrified. They didn't want golden cottages or peoples adulation! They were missionaries for Christ!

Tearing their clothes in distress, they declared their identity and purpose.

'We are but men. Turn to the living God!'

This should be the message of every true missionary of Christ! The crowds in Lystra, had little understanding of spiritual truths and were bound by fear and superstition.

Paul tried to direct them to the evidence of creation and conscience, as pointers to the true God, but their response had hardened into angry rejection. Then after the Jews from the synagogues in Antioch Pisidia and Iconium came and spoke to them, the people took Paul and began to stone him. This was the Jewish death sentence for blasphemy. All hell was uniting against the gospel of Christ; but it was the men of Lystra who actually threw the stones! Just as the Lord gives people spiritual vision for His divine purposes, Satan uses spiritually blind people in his.

Paul was dragged outside the city and left for dead but when some of the faithful converts came and gathered around him, he rose up again.

With real courage, but little alternative, they took him back into the city. Both Paul and Barnabas were brave men, but they were not foolish. Their missionary journey was not a holiday, or a hobby. Paul bore the scars of this encounter for the rest of his life, but he still continued his Christian witness in glorious victory.

The next day he went to another town called Derbe and preached to the crowds there. His physical experience of being stoned and left for dead, before being raised up, was in itself a pointer to the miraculous death and resurrection of the Lord Jesus. In response to his message, many people became Christians.

When they had finished in Derbe, Paul and Barnabas went back to the very towns where they had just been persecuted. They had Holy Ghost courage and a concern for the wellbeing of the new believers that they had left behind. Although they were itinerant preachers of the gospel, they weren't just 'hit and run' evangelists. When they spoke to these new converts, they reminded them of the challenges there would be to face.

'We must through many tribulations enter the kingdom of God.'

Salvation was by the grace of God, because of the work of Calvary, but living in the good of it would bring real opposition from unholy sources.

Paul and Barnabas appointed elders to care for the congregations in the churches they had pioneered, before beginning their journey back to Antioch in Syria, the starting point of their missionary outreach. Later Paul wrote in a letter to the Galatian believers,

'God forbid that I should boast, except in the cross of our Lord Jesus Christ, by whom the world has been crucified to me and I to the world.'

He went on to emphasize that they had not just changed their religion, but had received new life in Christ.

When he and Barnabas arrived in the city of Antioch, they told the church members there all that the Lord had done in bringing these new churches to birth among the Gentiles. They stayed there for about a year and enjoyed fellowship with the believers before another determined attack emerged against God's work. This time it was more subtle.

During His earthly ministry Jesus had warned the disciples of false teachers who would come as wolves dressed in sheep's clothing. A group of men came down to Antioch from Judea purporting to be Christian teachers. They questioned the very basis of salvation through faith in Christ alone and insisted that people must also be circumcised, in accordance with the Jewish law. The whole Christian message was being challenged. Satan was attacking again, but this time it was from within the growing church.

The whole doctrinal issue had to be made abundantly clear so that the gospel would not be hindered and Paul and Barnabas challenged these teachers of legalism and a false understanding of salvation. Then they agreed to go up to Jerusalem and meet with the other apostles and elders, in order that the whole issue could be clearly settled. In this way every believer in the future would know the purpose of God concerning the old Jewish law. This meeting would later become known as the council of Jerusalem. Such councils have been called to resolve church disputes all through the years, with varying degrees of benefit to the Christian message.

In 325AD Constantine, the Roman Emperor who had earlier become a confessing Christian himself, called three hundred bishops together to clarify the churches teaching on the person and work of Christ.

Presbyter Arius, from Alexandria argued that the Lord Jesus was not of the same nature and substance as God, but that He only became a son of God after His birth at Bethlehem. The Holy Spirit was more of a force than a person and therefore there was no Trinity. According to bishop Arius, Christ was only involved as an intermediary in the work of creation. Much of his teaching was like that of the Jehovah's Witnesses today.

Constantine held his council at Nicea and the Nicean creed was formulated as a worldwide confession of belief in the Trinity. People became Christians by the work and person of the Lord Jesus who, as Saviour, was sent from God the Father to give eternal life through the work and person of the Holy Spirit.

The Nicean creed did much to clarify doctrine, but with it came fresh challenges. Constantine's own part in its formation created problems. As the Roman emperor, Constantine made it acceptable and even politically advantageous to become a Christian.

This produced a considerable number of nominal believers without genuine conviction. Many of the buildings that had been used for the worship of Roman and other gods, became the places where church congregations met. The true church that Jesus had died to save was not a building made of material things, but was made of real people trusting in the work of Calvary and living in faith by the power of His Spirit.

Even today church committees can give many of their material resources, as well as their time and energy to constructing and maintaining elaborate buildings. Many of these can be visited as fine mausoleums, in memory of some former preacher, who died years previously. This is not the message of the gospel that Jesus commissioned His first disciples to take into all the world!

However, the first church council at Jerusalem was a necessity. Sound doctrine had to be clearly established so that the Christian message could be effectively proclaimed throughout the world.

When the apostles came together to consider the matter of circumcision, Peter was the first speaker. He spoke about the conversion of Cornelius, to whom he had preached of the Lord Jesus as the anointed, crucified and risen Son of God. The Holy Spirit had confirmed His own work with powerful signs and wonders happening among the uncircumcised Gentiles.

They had even experienced their Gentile Pentecost and began to praise God in tongues.

Paul and Barnabas then testified of how God had moved miraculously within the lives of the Gentiles when they had been on their missionary journey. How Bar-Jesus had been judged, how Sergius Paulus converted and the lame had been healed. Paul himself had been stoned and strengthened again. The Gentiles testimony was of salvation, not circumcision! The Lord Jesus had delivered them from their old religions and brought them to faith in the one true God.

Paul quoted from the Old Testament prophet Amos who had spoken about the restoring of King David's fallen tabernacle, so that all mankind, Jew and Gentile may seek the Lord. He was showing that the authority of scripture confirmed the work that had gone on in Antioch and in the Galatian churches.

Christ Himself had commissioned the disciples to take the gospel to all nations and He was now calling out a people for His own name. Christians were giving their allegiance to the Messiah, the Son of David and God was building His church that would last for eternity!

Under divine inspiration, Paul declared that things should not be made difficult for the Gentile believers by troubling them with unnecessary laws, but that they should be instructed to demonstrate their transformed lifestyle by turning from idolatry and immorality. These instructions for spiritual, moral and dietary purity, would bring encouragement and not offence to the genuine Jewish believers themselves.

The missionary message was neither about new buildings or old religious practices, but of a crucified and risen Saviour who had come because of God's love for all the world.

Chapter 10
The Expanding Witness

Trrue church growth is a demonstration of spiritual life and not simply a statistical increase. As God moved by His Holy Spirit in the New Testament church, a repeated fivefold pattern of events seemed to occur. God acted in sovereign grace and people responded in faith, then there was a supernatural confirmation of what had happened and the devil attacked the work God had done. Through all of these things, the church grew and demonstrated the victory of Christ over Satan.

When Paul and Barnabas returned to Antioch from the council of Jerusalem, they brought a letter from the apostles and elders in Jerusalem and read it to the church. A decision had been made fully acknowledging Gentile believers as Christians. Judas and Silas, men who had already been used in a prophetic ministry in Jerusalem, came to the church in Antioch and as a result, it was encouraged and strengthened. Even in the apostolic days, ministry in the local gathering of Christians was not the responsibility of one man.

Paul and Barnabas were men of Godly character, who served the Lord well together. Their natural temperaments had been complimentary in the work of the gospel. Human compatibility is good, but we need to be led by the Spirit of Christ and not just our own human reactions, for Satan can use even our own natural disposition towards his ends!

As the church in Antioch became stronger, Paul became more concerned for the new converts left behind in Derbe and Lystra and he suggested to Barnabas that they should return there to help them.

Paul probably had a choleric temperament. He had born the scars of conflict and was looking toward the end goal of seeing people saved and established in the worship of Christ, before the Lord returned to reveal His eternal kingdom.

Barnabas was a man of compassion, who had given encouragement where it was needed and had lived sacrificially for the glory of God. He had already helped the Christians in Cornelius's house and encouraged Paul himself. Now he wanted to give John Mark, his nephew, a fresh chance to serve the Lord with them, but Paul would have none of it. For him, it was a too big a risk to take John Mark with them. When he had deserted them previously he had proved himself to be unreliable. Feelings became heated and division followed. As a result Barnabas took John Mark and sailed to Cyprus and Paul took Silas with him as his partner in mission. Division had come between these early Christian missionaries.

Sometimes the devil seems to have won a victory, but Satan's tactics do not defeat the One who has promised to build His church! The division between Paul and Barnabas caused two missionary teams to go out with the gospel and the Word of God spread even further. Paul later spoke cordially about Barnabas and John Mark himself was used to record the gospel named after him when he acted as scribe for the apostle Peter.

Silas was suited for the challenge of ministering alongside Paul as he himself had been used in a prophetic teaching ministry. As a Jew he had access into the synagogues, and with Roman citizenship he had all the legal and cultural benefits this brought.

After the division with Barnabas the people in the church in Antioch sent Paul and Silas out with this message of salvation by grace to all who would respond. Travelling by land toward Derbe and Lystra they visited the churches that had sprung up in Syria and Cilicia.

When they arrived back in the Roman province of Galatia, in the town of Lystra, where Paul had been stoned, they met a young man called Timothy. His father, who had probably died some time previously, was a Greek and his mother was a Jewish believer in Christ. Following his own personal committal to faith in the Lord, Timothy was to become John Mark's replacement in the mission team. Later he was given the responsibility of leadership in the church in Ephesus. In a letter to the Corinthian believers Paul called Timothy, 'my son in the faith.'

When Timothy joined in testimony with the others, the very town of Lystra, the place of Paul's persecution for the gospel, had become the place of God's provision for his ministry!

Before they launched out as a team, Paul had Timothy circumcised. The message would be more effectively received if Timothy was accepted in the synagogues with his team partners. If he had not been circumcised the Jews would have thought he had denied his Jewish background and he would have not been received or allowed to speak in their gatherings. It was for the sake of the gospel and not for the sake of his salvation that Timothy was prepared to accept this rite.

God who can open doors of opportunity, can also shut doors according to His own purpose! While Paul and the team were trying to enter the Roman province of Bithynia, the Holy Spirit stopped them. When they were at the town of Troas, Paul lay down to sleep and during the night had a clear vision of a man from Macedonia, (Macedonia was an area on the Greek mainland) who was pleading with him to come and help them. In response to this vision, they sailed from Turkey, across to Greece and made their way to Philippi, a Roman colony. The missionary team had entered Europe for the first time! Philippi was a prosperous, self governed town, with special tax exemptions and land ownership rites, but it was still a place of real spiritual need. Down by the river, a wealthy business woman met with some of her friends to pray. Her name was Lydia. In her business, she made the expensive purple fabric used in making elegant clothing worn by the socially elite. She herself was an earnest and humble woman who went to meet with God by the river because there was not the required quorum of ten Jewish men to establish a local synagogue. God saw her heart and sent the message of salvation to where she was. As soon as she heard Paul speak about Jesus, she knew she was hearing the truth and she was baptised as a Christian.

There was no holding her back in her new found faith and she invited Paul and Silas to come and stay in her home. The first Christian church in Europe was born in the house of Lydia.

The Holy Spirit had led Paul and Silas to Philippi; God's word had been declared; Lydia had responded but then the devil's opposition became more antagonistic. His next insidious attack was immediately followed by confrontational aggression .

Firstly a young girl began to follow the evangelistic team shouting,

'These men are the servants of the most high God, who proclaim to us the way of salvation.'

Her message was true, but the motive behind the message was not. She was a medium who could tell fortunes, working for men who used her for their own nefarious purposes.

Her power wasn't from God, it was from the devil. The attention she had generated wasn't focused on Jesus, it was on herself and her spiritistic gifting. Straight away Paul discerned the source of her conduct and rebuked the spirit within her.

How the gift of discernment is needed today! Religious charlatans have not gone away! Deceiving spirits have not ceased from propagating their deceptions.

Paul addressed the spirit within the poor girl and commanded,

'In the name of Jesus Christ, come out of her!'

The spirit left but the people who used this slave girl for their own nefarious purposes were not pleased.

Her conduct had changed. She would no longer tell fortunes and their corrupt source of income had gone.

In fury they dragged Paul and Silas to the magistrates, falsely accusing them of starting a riot. They were stripped and beaten, thrown in prison and had their feet put in stocks.

The attraction of genuine Christian ministry has never been that of the material benefits! Throughout the centuries, believers have been tortured for their faith and martyrs have laid down their lives for the sake of the gospel, but God can deal with the power behind these things and He did that for Paul and Silas in a prison cell!

Lydia and the fellow believers in her house church would certainly have been praying.

At midnight, chained in the darkness, bleeding and in pain, Paul and Silas prayed and sang hymns of praise to the Lord. Sometimes people complain over something as simple as the church seats being too hard, but Paul and Silas who really were in dire straights simply worshipped God! This God whose message they were sharing with the people of Philippi, did care about the situation they were in. He heard their prayer of faith and answered it beyond their expectations. Locked in the darkness of the inner prison, with a Roman jailor outside the cell door, they heard a deep rumbling sound. The brackets holding the chains that bound them fell loose and the whole building began to tremble. Suddenly the full force of a mighty earthquake shook the very foundation of the building. Doors flew open, chains came off and the prisoners were at liberty! God had heard Paul and Silas's prayer and they were free; but they used this liberty to stay and not to escape! They knew that their lives were in their Saviour's hands and that they were on His business! They saw the jailor. He was a hard man. To become a jailor he had already served in the army and had probably seen men dying in pain. He knew what would happen to him if prisoners escaped while he was on duty. The execution of the guards who had failed to detain Peter was a stark reminder of the practises that went on across the Roman empire.

Taking a sword, he was about to commit suicide when Paul's voice rang out,

'Do yourself no harm! We are all here!'

Instead of fleeing from the prison they had shouted to the jailor.

He reached for a light: It was true, the prisoners were all there! - Why? -

God was building His church and he was going to be a part of it! Hallelujah!

'What must I do to be saved?'

Beyond their own spiritual opposition and personal suffering, Paul and Silas saw the God of their salvation at work in the jailor's life.

'Believe on the Lord Jesus Christ and you and your household will be saved!'

As the former Roman soldier asked Jesus to become his Lord and Saviour, his eternal destiny was changed and his own life was transformed.

Instead of locking up the prisoners again, he invited them to come to his house where they could eat and have their wounds treated. His whole family were amazed and they all were baptized as believing Christians. Going to Lydia's house they met with those gathered there.

God was building His church in Philippi!

Some twelve years later Paul wrote to its members again from house arrest and encouraged them to know true spiritual unity in Christ. He had been prepared to leave behind the privileges of his own upbringing, following the example of the Lord Jesus who had exchanged the comfort and adulation of heaven for the darkness of a cross in order to save him!

From prison in Rome, he instructed his readers to have the same attitude as his Saviour. Jesus had humbled Himself to come down into a sinful, suffering world to save people for eternity. He came down to a manger, to a cross, to a borrowed tomb, before He rose up from the grave, victorious over death and hell. Then He came into the lives of those who responded to God's gift of salvation and worked through them that others too may receive eternal life.

Because of the pride that many of the inhabitants of Philippi had in being Roman citizens, Paul emphasised the fact that the believer's true citizenship was in heaven itself. The Philippian Christians were journeying through their time on earth en route to their final heavenly destination. So is every true believer today!

Sometimes the journey can still be difficult, but Paul taught the Philippians about the God given joy that was real even in dire circumstances. Later from his prison cell in Rome he wrote to them,

'Rejoice in the Lord always. Let your gentleness be evident to all. Do not be anxious. Pray about everything, with thanksgiving. His peace will guard your hearts and minds.'

Paul was sharing the truth with them that he had proved in his own life. He and Silas had seen God both literally and spiritually

moving people and places in the town of Philippi! When the gospel
had been declared and church had been planted There it was time for
the missionary team to move on themselves. The Holy Spirit, who had
lead them to Macedonia to meet Lydia and the jailor and his family,
now led them to journey south west, past Amphipolis, (the former
capital of the area) and Appollonia (another town twenty seven miles
further on) towards Thessolonica. When they reached the actual town,
they entered the synagogue and explained how according to prophesy,
the Messiah had to die and be raised from the dead three days later.
Thessolonica was a busy commercial centre with about two hundred
thousand inhabitants. It was often called the 'mother of Macedonia.'

When he arrived there, Paul didn't preach about political
correctness, or some personality cult, or prosperity, or even about his
own God given abilities. He was absolutely certain in his declaration,

'This Jesus, whom I preach, to you is the Christ!'

For three weeks the gospel was powerfully declared and numbers
of men and women in the city accepted the saviour. Not only some of
the Jews in the synagogue, but large crowds of God fearing Greeks
recognised the truth of Paul's challenging words. Leading women in
the town came to faith and the church there was born in the power of
God. Across the various cultures, nationalities, social structures and
religious backgrounds the gospel of Christ had demonstrated the
purpose of God to save people for eternity.

Then the opposition came! The Jews who had been unwilling to
receive the truth were jealous of the effect that the ministry of Paul and
Silas was having. They hired some 'hit men' and started a riot.
Surrounding the house of Jason, a Jewish convert, they dragged him to
the city magistrates and accused the Christians of being trouble
makers.

'These people that have turned the world upside down have
come here also!'

Not a bad claim to make against missionaries who had been
whipped, beaten, imprisoned, contradicted and accused. The message
they brought truly did turn worldly values upside down, so that people
could stand the right way up and face Almighty God!

Because of his new faith Jason was taken to court, then released on bail before Paul and Silas were hustled from the city. Nevertheless, the Lord had worked in his heart and in the hearts of many others there. The radical stand they had to make strengthened them for the walk of faith that lay ahead!

The people opposing the Christians in Thessolonica had accused them of having another king beside Caesar. This was bad news in Rome, but the divine sovereignty of Jesus had been recognised by those folks who had responded to His message. They were not a political threat, they were part of an eternal kingdom!

Following the trouble in Thessolonica and probably aware that he was still in pain following the events in Philippi, the believers sent Paul to Berea where the people were more 'noble minded'. They didn't want him to endure unnecessary suffering. However wherever he went the message of Christ was his first priority.

Throughout the ages, counterfeits of and deviations from the truth, have plagued the church. Even in places of comparatively sound exposition of the Word, excessive emphasis on matters of personal doctrinal preference have brought imbalance and so inhibited the full declaration of the gospel. While humbly listening to God's word, the Bereans didn't simply swallow all that even the apostle Paul was saying, but they went to the scriptures, and confirmed the validity of his teaching. Paul's commendation of their action underlines its value and wisdom to every seeker of God!

When Paul wrote to the Thessalonian believers from Corinth, just a few months later he not only prayed for them but thanked God as well. They had been vigorous in their testimony despite the antagonism they had faced and they had been a powerful witness to many others. This witness spread even beyond their immediate geographical area.

'Your faith toward God has gone out, so that we do not need to say anything, for they themselves declare – how you turned to God from idols to serve the true and living God!'

In his letter to the Christians in Thessalonica he told them to be aware that Jesus would return to this earth to call them to be with Him in heaven. Each believer's spirit would have gone to be with the Lord the very moment it had left its earthly abode but at the Lord's coming those who died before His return would be given a new resurrection body, similar to the body He Himself had revealed after His own resurrection. The transformation of a caterpillar becoming a butterfly gives an imperfect, but helpful picture of this. Believers who will still be alive when the Lord returns will be taken to be with Him and changed in a moment into their eternal state.

The prophetic indications of the second coming of the Lord Jesus as the King of Glory, are recorded throughout scripture. His return will be announced by the trumpet of God and the voice of an archangel. Paul wanted the new Christians to live in both the comfort and the challenge of that fact. They had not to become indolent because of it, forsaking their daily responsibilities, neither had they to forget it and become taken up with the selfish temporal concerns of a pleasure seeking world..

Paul and Silas moved with an eternal vision but the believers in Thessolonica were living in one kingdom and belonging to another. Paul had warned them,

'The day of the Lord so comes as a thief in the night.'

To those who are deaf to the teaching of God's word, it will be without warning.

Someone has suggested that today as Christians we should plan as if we are going to live here forever but live in a way that is prepared for the Lord to return at any moment.

No man knows the day nor the hour of His return, but the prophetic evidences of scripture really are indicating that it will not be long.

The expanding witness of the Christian church will soon be an eternal expression of Christ's grace and power and glory!

Chapter 11
Greece

Christian ministry had not been a comfort zone for the apostle Paul! Jews from Thessalonica came to Berea to stir up riots against his testimony there. He was hounded out of Macedonia, even though he had been called of God to go into it- but he still left behind the living church of Christ!

Travelling on to Greece, he arrived at Athens, where he saw that the whole culture was dominated by idolatry. Man-made gods of silver and gold were worshipped by the credulous people. So called deities that had to be carried around on animals, or placated by obnoxious sacrifices, held the population in superstition and moral decadence. The gospel that Christ had sent Paul to share would set free from those things. Instead of men lifting idols up in decadence, the Saviour of sinners had come to lift up men and women in deliverance.

Today idolatry is much more sophisticated, but nevertheless it still leads people into bondage. Whether it is simply worshipping material possessions, or genuflecting before religious icons, the result is still the same: it robs people of a living relationship with the true God.

As well as idolatry, the vain philosophies that echoed around Athens brought a intellectual pride to its inhabitants. Some followed the teaching of Epicurus, who had been born in 341BC and believed that man's chief purpose was to avoid all pain and to live for his own pleasure. To the Epicureans, the gods were real, but passive and careless of their lifestyle. Their ambition was to 'eat drink and be merry, for tomorrow we die.' They denied that the gods had any involvement in the creation of the world and were just distant uninvolved spiritual entities.

The philosophers of Athens could also quote Zeno, the founder of Stoicism, who believed that men should be indifferent to either pleasure or pain. They should be self sufficient. The Stoics were Pantheists, believing that god was a part of everything. Selfishness and superstition were rife.

Even though the inhabitants of Athens were very religious, their spirituality was false. Hebrew culture gave every aspect of a man's life spiritual significance, whereas the Greek culture divorced the spiritual and the material, allowing him to believe a false religion and behave in unholy ways.

Almighty God does not desire religion, but rather a personal relationship with every individual who will respond to Him. That is why He sent His Son to be the Saviour of the sinners!

The Corinthians knew all the answers. The trouble was that they didn't understand the problem. Sin had cut people off from God and only the blood of Christ could re-establish that relationship. When that relationship is alive, the behaviour of every true believer in Jesus is transformed by the power of the Holy Spirit. For true Christians, their lives should be pleasing to God and a witness to others!

In an endeavour to reach these people where they were, both in their understanding and their conduct, Paul, highly intellectual himself, quoted from their own teachers while he was preaching in the market place.

When he referred to one of their various notices dedicated to the 'Unknown god,' his spirit burned within him to make the living God truly known!

Some of his listeners mocked him and asked, 'What does this babbler say?'

They literally called him a 'seed-picker,' believing that he was taking little snippets from their philosophers and not understanding what they really meant. Paul was provoked in his spirit by the situation in Athens, but he proved God as his strength and moved forty five miles west to Corinth to take the gospel there.

When he arrived, the situation looked even worse than the one that he had left! Corinth was the multi-racial, political, commercial centre of the region. The goddess Aphrodite was worshipped in a temple surrounded by a thousand cultic prostitutes and sailors. Temple worshippers were directed through the city to procure their services. Moral debauchery went under the disguise of religion, but in effect, this coarse immorality of Corinth was no worse than the proud intellectual sin of Athens! The eternal consequence of both would be the same!

It is amazing where the Lord Jesus has His people to be a witness of the one who is the way, the truth and the life! Not only had Paul gone to Corinth, but two Jewish believers were already there. Aquila and his wife Priscilla had been thrown out of Rome in 49AD in a pogrom led by the Emperor Claudius. They were probably Christians who had been in fellowship in the church that already existed in the capital city of the empire. As the owners of a tent-making, leather-working family company, they possibly had branches of their business in Rome, Corinth and Ephesus. When Paul arrived in Corinth, this was a 'God appointment' and he was able to work with them as a tent maker to provide material support for the Christian outreach in the city.

Shortly afterwards Silas and Timothy were prompted by the Holy Spirit to join with Paul in his new missionary endeavour. They had left behind the flourishing church in Thessolonica where they had remained when Paul had moved on and they also brought a financial gift from the church in Philippi. Practically and prayerfully these believers were all working together for the extension of God's kingdom! However the opposition had not gone away either. The precious little nucleus of the Christian working together in Corinth shared their faith with the Jewish worshippers in the synagogue, but it wasn't long before there was an antagonistic response. Paul preached in the power of the Spirit. He didn't rely on the vanity of man's wisdom, or on the attractions of material prosperity, but preached a Christ-centred message. His later letter to the church in Corinth declared its content.

'We preach Christ crucified, to the Jews a stumbling block and to the Greeks foolishness, but to those who are called, both Jews and

Greeks, Christ the power of God and the wisdom of God!'

Paul's powerful Saviour touched the lives of both, but some of the Jews in Corinth attacked his message in a blasphemous way and he left their synagogue with the warning,

'Your blood be on your own heads, I am clean. From now on I will go the Gentiles.'

Having fulfilled his responsibility to take the message of Christ to his own people first, he went to the house of a proselyte who lived next door to the synagogue and told him about Jesus. His name was Justus and he opened his home for the church to use. Then Crispus, one of the leaders from the synagogue, responded to the message and he with his family, joined with the Christians! When the Corinthians heard what was happening and what was being preached, many of them believed and were baptised as well! God was moving in power! In the middle of decadent Corinth, people were being delivered from Satan's clutches and saved from their sin! Heaven rejoiced, but hell was furious!

God spoke to Paul through another vision and told him not to fear the opposition, but to speak boldly, because there were many in the city who would respond to the gospel. So for the next eighteen months he preached from the Scriptures and saw the church increase in size and strength. However fresh opposition soon came in the form of another Jewish man called Sosthenes. He was a leader in the local community and in the synagogue. By this time it was 51AD. and Gallio was the Roman proconsul in the city. Sosthenes took Paul to court and charged him with forming an illegal religious gathering.

God's specific promise of divine protection proved true for Paul because when the court proceedings were convened before the judgement seat, on a large stone platform in the middle of the market place, Gallio dismissed the case as being a theological and not a legal issue. The Greek spectators arose in anti-Semitic rage and beat Sosthenes. His anger had rebounded on himself. This was not Paul's desire, he wanted all men everywhere to be saved and especially the Jews, but God had delivered him from this attack on the Lord's work through them.

The amazing thing was that God continued to work in Sosthenes heart and before long he became a believer himself! Throughout the world today, many Jews are recognising Jesus as their Messiah and receiving Him as their personal Saviour.

The grace of God that reached Sosthenes is still at work, melting hard hearts and converting rebels to be His witnesses, not just from the Jewish community, but from every nation under the sun!

The Corinthian church shone as a witness for God in a situation that was dark with sin! However, because of the decadent culture from which it was emerging, it needed firm instruction to understand the ways of the Lord. Paul later wrote three challenging letters to the believers there. These were sent to the saints in Corinth, from the apostle Paul and 'Sosthenes our brother.'

One got lost in history and another was written to the church and to Timothy, who had gone to serve the Lord there. The first epistle was written from Ephesus in 55AD to deal with the worldly conduct that was being allowed to go uncorrected in the assembly. Gross sins were bringing the church's reputation into disrepute. Paul's strong letter challenged those who brought shame to the gospel. He warned them about the severity of God's judgements, but also expressed the reality of God's grace. He challenged the spiritual apathy that allowed an incestuous relationship within the congregation to pollute it's witness to the world. Radical discipline was necessary! The man needed to be excluded from fellowship with God's people until he truly repented. Paul also warned the Corinthians of the dire consequences of partaking in the act of communion in an unworthy way;- spiritual and physical judgement would follow.

They had not only allowed people living in immorality to take part, but the very meeting to break bread and remember the Lord's death, had become a battlefield of selfish interests. Greed and contention had free expression. There was disorder in the meetings and Paul wrote to declare God's order. Corrective instructions were given to the believers concerning their celebration of the Lord's Supper.

In this city, where religious prostitution was rife, he instructed the women in the church to wear head-covering in order to honour the Lord and show their willingness to submit to His family order. Head-covering was an outward demonstration of the humble respect that these ladies had for the Lord as they prayed. Their lives were to be distinct from the sinful practises that went on around them in order to be a witness for Jesus.

Prayerful women had been used of God from the beginning of history.

Before Israel even had their first king, Hannah had prayed for the birth of a son. In answer to this Godly woman's prayer, the prophet Samuel had been born. His ministry had brought spiritual revival to the nation.

At the moment of the annunciation, Mary the Lord's mother had rejoiced in the prayer of the magnificat.

'My soul magnifies the Lord and my spirit has rejoiced in God my Saviour.'

The one who came to be Mary's Saviour is our Saviour today!

Mary had also been praying in the upper room with the other disciples on the day of Pentecost. She too received the baptism of the Holy Spirit.

Lydia, who had prayed at the riverside, before Paul had brought the gospel to Philippi, had then prayed in her house when the church was born and the believers gathered.

God wanted the members of the Corinthian church to be a people of prayer, but the prayers and conduct of the Christians in Corinth had to be very distinct from the conduct of the pagan worshippers around them. Paul warned them that participation in the Lord's supper in a way that was unworthy, would bring divine judgement. He encouraged the Christians to examine themselves and make sure that their motives and practise were pure. The institution of eating the bread and drinking wine to remember the Lord Jesus was a celebration of being set free from slavery to sin.

However his message to the church was still one of the grace of God towards sinners.

In another letter to the Corinthians, written shortly after he had left Ephesus, Paul instructed them to receive the man formerly involved in the incestuous relationship, back into the church. His expulsion from Christian fellowship and the disciplining of the Lord had brought him to true repentance. In the light of this, Paul urged them to reaffirm their love towards him. Their own lives were called to be living letters of the message of God's grace and purity.

Paul's letter reminded them that God had added to His church in Corinth, people who had been slaves but set free from sin. They had been perverts, thieves and bullies, but all of these been changed by the Saviours mighty power!

'Do you not know that the unrighteous will not inherit the kingdom of God? Do not be deceived; Neither fornicators nor idolaters, nor adulterers, nor sodomites, nor thieves, nor covetous, nor drunkards, nor revilers, nor extortioners will inherit the kingdom of God and such were some of you! You were sanctified! You were justified in the name of the Lord Jesus Christ and by the Spirit of our God!'

The power of the gospel had made the lives of these people pure and given them a purpose that was for time and eternity!

Even today defiance to God brings judgement, in social, material and national ways that are often unrecognised by a spiritually blind people. They treat the symptoms and placate the offenders! The true word of God doesn't excuse sin and explain it away, it exposes sin and calls to repentance! This was the nature of the epistle Paul wrote to the Corinthians. Nevertheless it was a powerful testimony that God should plant His church and commit the reputation of His Son to the people who were in the city of Corinth. The Lord works in the same way today as we allow scripture to speak to us and the Holy Spirit to empower our lives for His glory.

There will be a final day of judgement when Jesus returns, but until then, God will build His church with people saved from every kind of sin.

Supernatural spiritual gifts became not only a blessing but a problem to the Corinthian believers. Some looked on them as a fetish rather than as means to honour the Lord and to strengthen the church. Paul's letter encouraged them to desire and exercise the gifts of the Holy Spirit in such a way that they demonstrated Christ's love to the church and declared His word to the needy world. The characteristics of divine love that should be expressed in and through genuine Believers, were described in detail; -

Patience, kindness, contentedness, humility, politeness, unselfishness, purity, truthfulness, hope and endurance.

These attributes are the outworking of the life of the Spirit of Christ in a person who has turned from sin and selfishness.

Paul had also warned the Galatian church about the works of 'the flesh.'

Those 'works' referred to unrestrained selfish gratification of natural desires which are contrary to the fruit of the Spirit of Christ. The works of the 'flesh' are identified in the areas of sexual immorality, idolatry, occult practice, hatred, jealousy, uncontrolled anger, selfish ambitions, heresies, envy, murder, drunkenness, loose parties and similar demonstrations of un-Christ like living.

Whether in a Jewish, Macedonian or Greek culture, the consequence of living in these ways would result in exclusion from the kingdom of God.

When Paul wrote to the Galations, he not only warned them of the works of the flesh, but he spoke about the fruit of the Holy Spirit.

Real Christians are exhorted to live in a way that demonstrates the life of Christ. Only the power of the Holy Spirit in willing hearts can make this possible!

During his earthly ministry, Jesus had spoken to the woman of Samaria and told her that God was seeking those who would worship Him in spirit and in truth. He wanted her to know the liberty and power of the Holy Spirit so she could live in accordance with God's Word. Her response had been one of faith and she brought the challenge of faith in Christ to all who had known her. As she responded to the Saviour, her life was so radically changed, that many others were effected.

In the same way, worshipping the Lord in spirit and in truth brought Godly liberty and holy responsibility to the Christians in Corinth.

The blessing of the union of spiritual liberty and biblical order will always demonstrate the message of salvation in Christ to a needy world!

God's holiness and God's love were revealed at Calvary, where the punishment of sin was applied and sinners were forgiven. Forgiveness did not mean lack of discipline, as the early church had already witnessed in the case of unrepentant Ananias and Saphira. Despite the shortcomings of the church in Corinth and the wickedness of society there, the testimony of Christ was honoured. Paul's inspired teaching to the church of Christ was towards that end.

The Holy Spirit had used him and his companions to pioneer the church there, but he still cared deeply for the various other congregations where he had been involved.

After returning to Athens for a brief visit, Paul sailed from the Corinthian port of Cenchrea to Ephesus. From there he sailed to Caesarea, making his way back to the church that he had set out from in Antioch and then from there he returned to Jerusalem, in time for the celebration of the Feast of Passover.

This was the end of what has been called his second missionary journey. In effect, his life, as is the life of every true Christian believer, was one missionary journey from earth to heaven!

The Lord still speaks in the power of the Spirit through the Scriptures. True holiness and divine love are the evidence of the genuine work of His grace in individual lives.

This testimony of a living Saviour is still the greatest need of the world today!

It may be in different spheres and it may not be easy, but every Christian is called to be a messenger of the gospel.

Chapter 12
Spiritual Warfare

Ephesus was a strategic city in the Roman province of Asia. It was a centre of commercial, educational and political significance and as such, Paul under God's leading, had promised to return there with the gospel message. Other spiritual influences had held sway in the area for many years. A temple had been built in the city to the goddess Diana whose image had supposedly fallen from the sky in the form of a meteorite. Many idols were made of her in the form of a multi-breasted woman, with lions in attendance. She was a 'virgin goddess' waited on by eunuch priests. However, as is often the case with spiritual deception, her worship was entwined with sexual impurity. The temple itself was an impressive structure, supported by one hundred sculptured columns of stone.

In 52AD a Jewish man who came from the old Egyptian seaport of Alexandria had gone there after Paul had left. He had a profound knowledge of scriptures and had received some basic teaching about Jesus, but he did not fully understand the significance of Christ's purpose and power. His name was Apollos and he had been baptised by John in the river Jordan, but he had never heard of the Holy Spirit. As an eloquent speaker he began to teach the people in Ephesus what he did know about the Lord. God was still at work building His church with all who would respond to His word. When Aquila and Priscilla were in the city, they heard Apollos preaching. Patiently they shared further details of the gospel message with him and as a result he immediately went to tell others. His ministry encouraged the believers and challenged the orthodox Jews, by pointing to the Lord's fulfilment of the Messianic promises in the Old Testament.

After visiting Jerusalem and then spending a few more months with the church in Antioch, Paul set out on his third missionary journey in the year 53AD. He travelled across Galatia and Phrygia, modern day Turkey, to visit the churches that had been planted there.

When he completed the fifteen hundred mile journey and came back to Ephesus, Apollos was away in Corinth. Finding new disciples in Ephesus, Paul immediately asked them,

'Did you receive the Holy Spirit when you believed?'

They had only heard of John's baptism of repentance, but wanted to receive the Spirit of the Lord Jesus and to be baptised in His name. When Paul prayed and laid hands on these new Christians, the Spirit of God came upon them in the same way He had on the disciples in the upper room in Jerusalem! About twelve men began to speak in other tongues and prophesy right there in Ephesus. The ongoing, empowering work of the third person of the Trinity was still effective in people's lives enabling them to obey Christ's command to be witnesses of the gospel. It still is! With divine authority Paul went into the synagogue and spoke boldly about the Lord for the next three months. God had given a wonderful opportunity for the message of salvation to be declared in a place of spiritual confusion and pollution.

However the encouragement of being involved in God's work did not remove the necessity of dealing with Satan's counter attacks! A message came from the church in Corinth reporting division among the members. Some claimed to be following Paul, some Apollos, some Peter and some Christ. This danger of following human preferences or a man-centred ministry has been a problem right throughout history: People have followed strong natural leadership and often gone in ways that have not brought glory to the Lord Jesus. The apostle Paul dealt with the situation in Corinth, clearly and immediately.

'Is Christ divided? Was Paul crucified for you? Were you baptized in the name of Paul?'

He continued saying,

'God has chosen the foolish things of this world to put to shame the wise and God has chosen the weak things of the world to put to shame the things which are mighty!'

He asked a rhetorical question and then gave them the answer,

'Who then is Paul, Who is Apollos?' – They were just servants who God used!

'I planted,' Paul said, 'Apollos watered; but God gave the increase!'

Their identity was to be found only in the crucified and risen Christ, their God-given Saviour! They were God's field, God's building!

So under the inspiration of the Holy Spirit, Paul had sent divinely given instructions to deal with Satan's attack on the church in Corinth; but in Ephesus, he faced yet another one right where he was situated.

Jesus had told His disciples that He was the way, the truth and the life that led to God the Father. In Ephesus, where the believers were called 'Followers of the Way,' the Jews who had resisted the gospel, began to slander them. After teaching in the synagogue for three months, Paul was thrown out yet again and the Christians moved the meeting into the lecture hall of a man called 'Tyranus,' whose name actually meant 'Little tyrant.' Perhaps it was a nickname.

It is amazing to consider some of the places where the church of Christ has met throughout history: Synagogues, workshops, prisons, ships, houses, on hillsides and even in the Roman catacombs!

The Ephesian church congregated in the hall of Tyranus during the afternoon break, between eleven in the morning and four o'clock in the afternoon. This was during the hottest time of the day when the premises were normally unused. Paul's practise of working as a tentmaker during the morning and speaking daily in the afternoons, continued for two years.

True Christian ministry is a vocation, not a vacation and as Paul fulfilled his divine calling to preach to the Gentiles, God confirmed his ministry with extraordinary signs. The Holy Spirit moved in his work place and the handkerchiefs that were used as sweatbands as well as the aprons used for working there, were taken to sick and demonized people who were healed and delivered when they touched them.

However Satan sent his counterfeits. Itinerant Jewish exorcists using a pseudonym, called themselves the 'Sons of Sceva, the High Priest. They tried to exorcise demons by calling on what they considered to be a more potent spiritual being and used the name of Jesus as a superstitious token.

Confronting a demonized man, they declared,

'We exorcise you by the Jesus whom Paul preaches!'

They commanded the unclean spirit to come out of the man but the spirit responded to them,

'Jesus I know and Paul I know; but who are you?'

With that the possessed man set about the group, stripping and injuring seven of them!

News about this spread throughout Ephesus and the people were frightened. Jesus had warned His disciples that there would be many superstitious charlatans around. He said that it would be especially so in the last days before He returned. His warning is more relevant today than it has ever been!

The Deceiver had tried to undermine Paul's ministry, but he had only damaged his own evil practises, for the new Christian believers brought their old occult literature and confessed and repented of their involvement with the evil arts. The material they brought was worth about fifty thousand pieces of silver, the equivalent of a years wages for one hundred and fifty men! It was all burnt. Their repentance was not shallow or cheap and as a result lives were changed by the power of God. Instead of participating in paranormal activities, people proclaimed what the Lord had done for them. Because of all of that had happened in the city, the name of Jesus was magnified.

Luke wrote, 'So the word of the Lord grew mightily and prevailed!'

As the church grew, Paul's own missionary vision was continually expanding and perhaps his own faith was growing too. He had been called to be a missionary to the Gentiles and now he wanted to reach the whole Roman empire! Having just witnessed the power of the Lord working so remarkably, he told the others that he was going back to Jerusalem via Macedonia to visit the new churches there, before heading to Rome itself. Paul was a man of intellectual ability, practical skill and spiritual passion and he would have been aware of the dangers that lay ahead in Jerusalem and known that only the Lord who had originally called him could enable him to fulfil his desires. He was sensitive to the Holy Spirit's leading, but he also made constructive plans and sent Timothy and Erastus, another believer, before him to Macedonia, while he stayed for a little longer in Ephesus.

About this time Demetrius, a silversmith who made images of the pagan goddess Artemis who was also known as Diana, began to make trouble for the Christians. Diana and Artemis may have been different names, but they represented the same grotesque unclean spirit. Demetrius's business of making idols had been severely restricted by the gospel and so he claimed that the whole economic climate of the town had been effected. Satan had stirred him to oppose the work of the Holy Spirit and he was angry as Paul preached the message of deliverance from evil. His reactions were not only because his pagan prosperity was being threatened, but because the population of hell was being restricted by the message of salvation and the devil himself was angry. He used Demetrius to whip the crowd up into a frenzy and they grabbed Giaus and Aristarchus, two of Paul's companions and dragged them into the theatre that seated twenty four thousand people. The mob rushed into the building, not really understanding what was happening. When they were there they shouted for two solid hours,

'Great is Diana of the Ephesians.'

Paul wanted to go in to be with his fellow Christians and try to pacify the crowd, but he was advised not to do so by some of the other disciples and also by the non Christian mayor of the town who had become his friend.

In his letter to the church in Corinth Paul told them that the missionaries had despaired of their very lives when they had been in the Roman province of Asia. When he wrote from a Roman prison to the church in Ephesus in about 61AD, he instructed the Christians about spiritual warfare. What had happened in their city wasn't simply social unrest, it was spiritual conflict.

'For we do not wrestle against flesh and blood, but against principalities and powers, against the rulers of the darkness in this age, against spiritual hosts of wickedness in the heavenly places.'

Demonic conflict is universal, regional and personal.

Paul wrote to them about the amazing purpose that Almighty God had, not only for the church in Ephesus, but for the church throughout the world and throughout time.

Before Christ came, this purpose had been hidden, not only from Godly folk under the old covenant, but from Satan himself.

Then in his letter to the Ephesians, Paul openly declared,

'To me who am less than the least of all the saints this grace was given that I should preach among the Gentiles the unsearchable riches of Christ and to make everybody see what is the fellowship of the mystery which from the beginning of ages has been hidden in God, who created all things through Jesus Christ, to the intent that now, the manifold wisdom of God may be made known by the church to principalities and powers in the heavenly places, according to the eternal purposes which He accomplished in Christ Jesus our Lord.'

Satan had been defeated at Calvary. Spiritual life had been given to Jew and Gentile alike because of the work done on the cross. The church was being called to demonstrate the spiritual victory of Christ on earth to every demonic power that opposed them.

Nations had been bound by principalities and powers from hell and Paul was revealing that Christ had come to set them free through the gospel given to the church. The power and authority of this was in Christ alone and the work would only be complete when He returned to deal with Satan for eternity. Until then the church has been given spiritual authority to rebuke demonic power and to declare the eternal gospel.

No wonder there was and is opposition!

Paul had been persecuted when declaring his message. Christians throughout the ages have suffered and been martyred for this message, but one day it will be gloriously fulfilled and heaven and earth will rejoice afresh in what the Lord has done.

In order to fulfil his ministry, Paul knew that he personally needed divine strength from his prayer-answering Saviour. He also prayed that the Ephesian believers would be strengthened with might in their inner man, so that Christ would dwell in their hearts through faith. Inner strength is still the gift of God's love in a world that is shaking apart!

In his letter he gave instructions on how to equip themselves for this kind of warfare;- how to be strong in the Lord and stand against the wiles of the devil.

'We do not wrestle against flesh and blood, but against principalities and powers, against the rulers of the darkness of this age and against spiritual hosts of wickedness in the heavenly places'

In the battle with the principalities and powers of hell, Paul began with prayer. He spoke about using the 'gospel armour' and drew the picture from the equipment used by a Roman soldier. The belt around the soldiers waist held everything together. Paul spoke about the 'belt of truth.' Satan is the father of lies, but Jesus had said, 'I am the Truth.' Openness with God brings the blessing of fellowship with other believers. Being real with the Lord and with one another, still holds everything together.

'Stand therefore, having girded your waist with truth, having put on the breastplate of righteousness and having shod your feet with the preparation of the gospel of peace; above all taking the shield of faith with which you will be able to quench all the fiery darts of the wicked one and take the helmet of salvation and the sword of the Spirit, which is the Word of God, praying always with prayer and supplication in the Spirit.'

The breastplate guarded the heart. The heart is not only a pump that enables the blood to circulate a persons body, but it is figuratively described as the very centre of the emotions. A believer must be guarded about what he or she set their heart upon. True righteousness gives emotional wisdom.

'Have your feet shod with the gospel of peace.'

Shoes are for walking in! Like the righteous prophets of old, every true believer should go where the word of God sends them and not simply where their fancy takes them!

The good news of knowing peace with God should bring direction in life.

'Take the shield of faith.'

In conflict on the battlefield, the shield would protect the soldier against the sword, spear and fiery arrows of the enemy. In spiritual conflict the attacks and accusations of the enemy of our soul can come in many injurious ways, but the shield of faith can and will deflect and protect. It will be able to quench all the fiery darts of the wicked one.

The suggestions and accusations of the enemy should simply not be received, they should be refused and refuted in faith. Satan seeks to wound with doubt and fear, in order to put God's people out of action. He brings temptation and condemnation, not conviction and restoration. He brings discouragement and despair, not vision and faith. The Roman shield had ridges around its edges which could be linked together with the shields of other soldiers on the battle front. This unity in action brought added protection. Although the shield of faith is personal, the fellowship of the saints in witness and prayer strengthens faith and is a powerful protection against the enemy of the soul.

'Take the helmet of salvation.'

The helmet guards the brain and the senses; What we hear, what we see, what we touch, what we taste, what we say, even what we smell. How important it is for every Christian to be wise in these areas. If we feed our body on the wrong food or drink, we will not be healthy. Paul later wrote to the Roman Christians and told them to present their bodies as a living sacrifice in worship to God. Our bodies are the temple of the Holy Spirit!

If we feed our mind with unsuitable material, our thinking will be polluted.

Someone has said, 'What we feed our minds on, we become.'

We are called to be transformed by the renewing of our minds.

'The sword of the Spirit, which is the word of God.'

Like the Ephesians, we are called to study and know scriptures not simply as an academic exercise, but in order to hear the Lord speaking into our lives. The authority of God's word presents the final case against the whispering voices of unrighteousness that permeate a world under Satan's influence. The Lord calls us to know His word and to know how to use it.

'Pray in the Spirit.'

Answered prayer will bring divine direction against the opposition and display the glory of the Lord.

Paul's wrote to the Ephesians and gave them instructions about the gospel armour, so that they would know the victory in Christ in their lives.

The Christian's spiritual armour is God's provision for every believer throughout history and it needs to be used more than ever today.

There is no victory without conflict, but the triumph of the cross is as real as it ever has been and will be so for all eternity.

In Ephesus, the opposition was frenzied, but the Almighty was in control! He still is.

Chapter 13
Resurrection Ministry

The mayor of Ephesus had managed to quieten the crowd and bring a degree of order into a dangerous situation. As a result Paul was able to leave the city and go back to Macedonia and minister to the believers there. His own comfort was very low on his list of priorities. Three months later he returned to Greece. This time the Jews plotted against him, so he went by land back to Philippi, where he met with Dr Luke, before sailing to Troas. He may have still been contending with some of the after effects of the physical attacks which he had suffered during his ministry, but the God who was the strength and purpose of his life had enabled him to be valiant in this battle for the salvation of men and women. His concern was that they might know the power and purity of a risen saviour for themselves and then to live for His glory.

When he and Luke arrived in Troas, they joined with their travelling companions who had gone on before and agreed to rendezvous with them there. This was the very place where Paul had received his initial 'Macedonian call.' It was near the old city of Troy, with its story of the Trojan horse. Troas itself had been named after Alexander Troas, also known as Alexander the Great. It had then became a Roman colony under Augustus and eventually was twinned with Rome. As a busy Mediterranean sea port, Julius Caesar had considered transferring the administrative centre of the empire to Troas. It was a city of historical renown, where political kingdoms had been fashioned.

Now, a humanly insignificant little group of Christians had gathered with Paul, in an upstairs room, to speak about an eternal kingdom!

Rather than on the Sabbath, which was the last day of the week, the believers at Troas met on the first day of the week. In the new covenant, which had been declared on the night of the last supper, Jesus had told His disciples to remember Him when they broke bread together. Under the old covenant, the Sabbath day had been specified as the religious day of rest. The new covenant enabled people to cease from attempting to please God through religious rituals and enter into a rest of faith through their relationship with the One who had fulfilled all righteousness. Christians began to meet on Sunday's after the resurrection. After creation, God had rested on the seventh day of the week; but Jesus had risen on the first day. He had appeared to grieving Mary outside the tomb on the first day. He had challenged and encouraged the despondent disciples on the Emmaus road on the first day. He had appeared to the disciples in an upper room in Jerusalem, then breathed His Spirit upon them and given them the commission to go into all the world with the gospel on the first day of the week. In his revelation of the risen Saviour, John was 'In the Spirit on Lord's day on the Isle of Patmos. It was the first day of a new week. Christ came first in all things.

Jesus had fulfilled the law and salvation was through faith in Him alone.

His fulfilment of the law was not to satisfy the hypocrisy of Rabbinic traditions, but to satisfy a holy God and to demonstrate the order that had been given for man's blessing.

After Pentecost, the, 'Thou shall NOT,' had become 'Thou SHALL not.'

Keeping the Decalogue was not the means of earning spiritual merit, but as the Old Testament prophets had foretold, the law which had been written on tablets of stone, had now been written on the hearts of real believers. They desired to please God in every way.

During His earthly ministry, Jesus had answered the querying scribe who had asked which of the commandments was the greatest:

'Love the Lord your God with all your heart, with all your soul, with all your mind.'

Then He had continued,

'You shall love your neighbour as yourself.'

Paul, in his letter to the Roman believers informed them,

'He who loves another has fulfilled the law.'

This love which was a fulfilment of the law was not antinomian in character, but holy.

On the first day of the week the new Christian believers met in the upper room in Troas to break bread in communion and to hear God's Word expounded by the apostle.

It was late. People had been working all day and they were tired, but they were putting Christ first. Paul had much to say. He was only with them for twenty four hours and in order to use the time purposefully, he had preached till after midnight. He expounded the scriptures and he declared what the Lord had done. It wasn't a twenty minute, alliterated semonette with visual aids and illustrations. The room was crowded and the heat from the flickering candles added its warmth to that of the massed body temperatures. One of the congregation was a young man called Eutychus. He was using a windowsill for a seat but his concentration was flagging as he began to feel his overwhelming tiredness.

Paul preached on and Eutychus nodded off! Suddenly he slumped over backwards and fell through the open window and down three stories onto the street below. When his body crashed to the ground, he lay silent. With desperate concern, people from the upper room rushed down and lifted him up; but he was motionless. Luke the physician had witnessed all of this and recorded his death. Immediately Paul came and embraced the young man, identifying with him in his need. His embrace wasn't just one of worried sympathy; he was trusting God to deal with the situation! As he threw his arms around Eutychus, Almighty God got powerfully involved! The words that Paul had shared with the people in Troas had spoken of a risen Saviour and now this ministry was confirmed in living power! Eutychus stirred and Paul spoke,

'His life is in him!'- Eutychus was alive!

They all went back upstairs into the upper room and Paul's sermon continued until dawn! God still can heal and He does answer prayer. The ministry of Christ, didn't only bring identification, it demonstrated resurrection! Eutychus had known a physical reviving from the dead, but Jesus had risen with a resurrection body, never to die again. He is the first born from the dead with an eternal body. Christians alive today will have to wait for that final resurrection morning when the Lord returns, before they completely shake off all of the aches and pains of living in a fallen world and go to be with the Lord in the place where there is no more death, nor sorrow, nor crying, nor pain. However, whether people are physically weak or strong, the Lord Jesus can bring inner revival in accordance with His Word, to all who fully respond to His Holy Spirit and in His sovereign purpose, He can still heal sick bodies today!

In 61AD, near the end of his life's ministry, Paul wrote from a prison cell in Rome,

'For me to live is Christ and to die is gain!'

He was looking forward to the day of his own resurrection, but living in the present day power of his risen Lord. The promise given, that even through suffering, he would be a witness to the Gentiles, was being fulfilled in the power of the Holy Spirit.

The day after his visit to Troas, Paul's companions went by ship around to the other side of a narrow peninsula to land at the port of Assos, twenty miles further south. Rather than sail with them Paul had chosen to walk the more direct route across the land and meet them there. When he rejoined them, he boarded the vessel and they sailed past the Greek island of Chios, where the poet Homer had been born. Then they sailed past Samos, the birthplace of the famous mathematician Pythagoras.

As a highly educated man, Paul had learnt the value of scholarly learning and often used his knowledge and reasoning powers for the sake of the gospel. However these benefits, along with his religious and social background were counted to be of no worth in gaining his spiritual life in Christ and he was prepared to be counted a fool for his

Saviour's sake. He gloried in the fact that the Lord often chose the weak and foolish people of the world to reveal God's power and wisdom. All of his own ministry was based on the grace of God, rather than the grandeur of the worldly achievements. The goals that he had in his life were for Christ's honour and not his own and yet he had seen the Lord moving powerfully as he ministered to others. During his missionary outreach, people had been healed and others judged, demons had been cast out and prison walls broken down, people had been forgiven and chosen to live holy lives, churches had been born and Jesus had been worshipped. Now he was on his way back to Jerusalem, again intending to be there on the day of Pentecost.

The vessel sailed past Ephesus and docked at Miletus, thirty miles to the south.

He sent a message to the elders of the Ephesian church and they came to meet him. Paul reminded them of the credentials of his ministry. He didn't mention his academic record or show them a framed diploma, he pointed to the testimony of his life and who it was that he served.

'You know from the first day that I came to Asia in what manner I always lived among you, serving the Lord with all humility, through tears and trials which happened to me by plotting of the Jews; How I kept nothing back from you that was helpful, but proclaimed it to you and taught you publicly from house to house, testifying to Jews and also to Greeks, repentance towards God and faith towards the Lord Jesus Christ.'

The prophets of the Old Testament had been divinely warned that if they did not faithfully deliver the full message of God to the people, the people's blood would be upon their shoulders.

Paul had been faithful in his responsibility to tell the Ephesians the truth, the whole truth and nothing but the truth! He said to the men who were listening to him,

'Therefore I testify to you this day that I am innocent of the blood of all men; For I have not shunned to declare to you the whole counsel of God.'

Then he went on to warn them of people who would come among them with false ministries,

'Take heed to yourselves and to all the flock, among which the Holy Spirit has made you overseers, to shepherd the church of God, which He has purchased with His own blood, for I know this, that after my departure savage wolves will come in among you, not sparing the flock. Also from among yourselves men will rise up, speaking perverse things to draw away the disciples after themselves.'

Carnal, self centred ministries have deceived people throughout history and have brought gullible people into bondage. In the final days of history this tendency will culminate in a universal delusion. Christ centred, Spirit-filled ministry has brought liberty into people's lives throughout history. At history's conclusion, the One who initiated that ministry will bring eternal deliverance.

The elders at Ephesus had been warned and it was their responsibility to be watchful. Paul reminded them that he had not coveted anyone's silver or gold, but that he had in fact worked with his own hands to support himself. He knew the truth of Christ's own teaching that it was more blessed to give than receive.

Even though Paul was aware that his work in Ephesus had been completed and that he was heading to Jerusalem where there would be imprisonment and tribulation, his goal was to finish his ministry with joy. When he had given his instructions to the Ephesian elders and prayed with them, the tears flowed. As they hugged one another, they knew that they would never meet again this side of eternity.

The ongoing journey involved changing ships at another busy port and then passing Cyprus and landing at Tyre. In this port Paul and his companions stayed with Christians who were already there and through them, he was warned again by the Holy Spirit of the consequences of what would happen if he went to Jerusalem. The Christians there included those who had been scattered from Jerusalem after Stephens martyrdom. As they opened their home to Paul and his friends they must have heard of his dramatic conversion and marvelled at God's amazing grace.

Setting sail again, another stop was made in the port of Caesarea, where Philip the evangelist lived with his four daughters all of whom had the gift of prophesy. It was a spiritual home and as the travellers stayed there, another prophet called Agabus came to stay. He took Paul's own belt and bound his hands and feet, warning him that the Jews would do that to him in Jerusalem, before handing him over to the Gentiles. Everybody pleaded with him not to go to the city, but Paul answered,

'What do you mean by weeping and breaking my heart? For I am not only ready to be bound, but to die for the name of the Lord Jesus.'

It was no flimsy, ephemeral faith that motivated the apostle; it was not self interest; he was on a mission to bring the message of eternal life to all who would hear.

The group in Philip's home bowed before the Lord and prayed, 'Your will be done.'

When the team eventually arrived in the capital they were welcomed by the believers there and the next day Paul reported to them what the Lord had been doing on his missionary journeys. James and the other church elders listened with great attention.

It must have been marvellous, hearing how the gospel message had been changing lives throughout the Roman empire. The Jerusalem church would have remembered the crucifixion and the commission that the Lord had given them with fresh understanding. The church that had begun as a little group of fearful disciples hidden in an upstairs room were now seeing the promises of Almighty God being outworked in a way that was reaching out across the Roman empire with the only message that could change the world! They glorified God, but immediately true faith came under attack again and Paul had to answer false charges of anti-semitic practise. He was a Jew who had recognised his Messiah and enjoyed the privilege of understanding that the prophesies and types of scripture had been fulfilled in Jesus.

Now he just wanted his fellow Jews to see this for themselves.

In humility, Paul followed James suggestion to pay for the expenses of four men who had taken a Nazarite vow and accompany them to Jerusalem during the seven days set aside for their purification. Because it was the feast of Pentecost, some Jews from Ephesus had come to the temple to celebrate both the first fruits of the harvest and the giving of the law to Moses. When they saw Paul, they shouted out, accusing him of defiling the place. This started an uproar and he was seized and then dragged out into the streets, where they tried to kill him. When a Roman commander saw what looked like a riot, he came to investigate and then arrested Paul as the troublemaker.

However when Paul was taken to the barracks for investigation, he spoke to the commander in Greek and after giving his identity asked for permission to address the crowd. He spoke to them in Hebrew, but didn't even mention their charges against him. Instead, he shared his own testimony with them. He told them of the call of God and of how Christ had sent him to take the gospel to the Gentiles.

When they heard him mention his mission to the Gentiles they were furious. His words stung them to the heart. They seemed like blasphemy to them and they tore their clothes and shouted.

'Away with such a fellow from the earth for he is not fit to live!'

They said that about Jesus, they responded like that to Stephen and now they wanted to kill Paul. The Roman officer had lost patience and he wanted to know the truth quickly, so he ordered him to be brought to the barracks and scourged so that he could get to the bottom of the matter.

As the soldiers were in the act of binding Paul in preparation to be whipped, he called out to the centurion who was standing near by,

'Do you have the legal rights to scourge an uncondemned Roman citizen?'

The centurion reported this to his commander, who immediately asked Paul for himself if he really was a Roman citizen. When the Roman went on to say that his own citizenship had cost him a lot of money Paul in answer declared,

'But I was born a citizen.'

This put his situation in a completely different context as Roman citizens had protection throughout the empire and were treated with respect.

The next day when Paul was allowed to face his accusers he began by telling them that his conscience was clear before God.

Immediately, Ananias, the High Priest from the temple ordered him to be struck across the mouth. Paul flared up in anger as he responded to him,

'God will strike you, you whitewashed wall! For you sit to judge me according to the law and do you command me to be struck contrary to the law?'

Ananias was an evil man with a vindictive spirit and he was judged by his own people some time later when he was murdered in a revolution against the Romans occupiers whom he supported. He had the eternal judgement of the Almighty to face after that. However when Paul was challenged about speaking to the High Priest in such a way and he apologised, saying that he was not aware that it was the High Priest. Ananias was a self righteous, religious hypocrite full of bitterness, but Paul respected his office and left the outcome in God's hands. He knew that he himself had been as bad as Ananias and that the Lord was well able to deal with such people. It was only God's mercy that had saved him and only His grace that saves people still.

However, when he saw that the court was made up of Pharisees and Sadducees, who normally were antagonistic to each other in political, social and theological understanding, he declared,

'I am a Pharisee, the son of a Pharisee; concerning the hope of the resurrection of the dead I am being judged.'

The Pharisees believed this and the Sadducees didn't, so his accusers turned on one another with Paul in the middle of it. The result was chaos.

The commander ordered him to be brought back into the barracks and that night the Lord spoke to him again.

'Be courageous Paul, you have testified for me in Jerusalem, so you must also bear witness at Rome.'

The word of God that speaks through the daily study of the scriptures can also speak with divine authority into our personal circumstances.

Some of the Jews whom Paul had offended, were so antagonistic towards his message that they vowed to kill him. Their plan was to set up another judicial enquiry, call him to attend it and then arrange an ambush to murder him en-route to the court. Paul's own family had previously rejected him because of his message, but God's word must have reached some of them, for his nephew came and warned him of this plot. This young man knew his uncle Paul's position and the price that he had paid with his own reputation, but his own heart was drawn to identify with him. He is not heard of again, but the Lord used him to save his uncle's life. What a joy to know that the Lord did and can work in desperate situations! At the end of his later letter to the Roman believers Paul included greetings to his relations, Andronicus, Junia, Herodian and Sosipater. Although these were unlikely to have been members of his immediate family, they were fellow Jews who lived in Rome and acknowledged the Lord Jesus.

The assassins had intended to kill Paul on the following day, but it was not in God's plan to allow it. Paul was ready to meet his Saviour, but he still had work to do on earth. He was busy in the Master's service. The Lord was building His church with real hands-on, face-to-face people and situations on planet earth, in the Roman empire and on the streets of Jerusalem. The apostle was one of His workmen! His message was not about a religious system, but a personal relationship with the living Saviour.

In the light of the plot against Paul's life, Lysias the commander, ordered two officers with four hundred and seventy military men to take him to be examined by Felix, the governor in Caesarea (the capital of the Roman province.) He sent an accompanying letter telling Felix about the plot against the life of the Roman citizen. Five days later when Ananias, the High Priest and his other accusers arrived, Paul stood before the governor and answered his questions, but judgment of the case was postponed until Lysias came to Caesarea. During the waiting period Paul challenged Felix and his wife Drusilla with the gospel. He spoke about righteousness, self control and judgement to come.

The governors wife was a Jewish girl of nineteen, whom he had seduced from her previous husband. She was his third wife. Felix's own background was one of slavery. He knew about the followers of 'The Way,' he knew Ananias was crooked and he knew that Paul had a clear conscience but he would not respond personally to God's message of forgiveness and eternal life. Paul had stood on trial before him, but now Felix was standing before the challenging testimony of God's word. He procrastinated. He put things off, because he knew what it would cost him.

'Go away for now. When I have a convenient time I will call for you.'

The worldly man who acted tough and treated Paul with disdain, was unwilling to face spiritual truth.

Paul was under house arrest and Felix sent for him many times during his next two years, but his only motive was to extract a bribe. At the end of this period, he died in office. His wife never came back to hear the gospel testimony.

Paul had witnessed to the good, the bad and the indifferent. They had all needed Jesus, but in order to receive Him they had all needed to respond to the message.

The dangers of procrastination can have eternal consequences!

Luke visited Paul while he was under house arrest and learned many facts from him that would later be recorded in his account of the life of the early church. Both of these men followed the leading of the Holy Spirit to bring God's word to a needy world. The message that they shared is as relevant today as it ever has been, for God is still speaking through His word by the power of His Holy Spirit.

Two years after that, Festus succeeded Felix as governor. Unlike his predecessor, whose background was that of slavery, he came from the Roman nobility. Nevertheless, his standing in God's sight was just the same, for he too was a slave to sin, needing to repent and know a God given salvation in Christ. He was a brutal man, who had suppressed a riot in Caesarea in such a way that the Jews living there had even complained to the Emperor Nero. He had been recalled to

Rome and would have been removed from his position if it hadn't been for the influence of his aristocratic family. Now when he came back to the province, he tried to ingratiate himself with the people by keeping Paul under arrest.

When Festus went up to Jerusalem the chief priest and his friends schemed to deal with the apostle Paul once and for all. Another plot was made to take his life.

They asked that Paul be taken back to Jerusalem so that en route another assassination squad would finally murder him. They had wanted to kill him for a long time because of his preaching about the message of eternal life. Unlike the governor, Paul's motive was not to gain popularity or prosperity, but to proclaim the truth. Festus told those wanting to question him to come to Caesarea themselves and he could be tried there. Grudgingly they came and made their complaints against him in court, but he was obviously not guilty. In order to please the High Priest, Festus asked Paul if he would be willing to go to Jerusalem to be tried there.

Paul knew what the corrupt outcome of that would be and refused by exercising his right as a Roman citizen.

'I appeal to Caesar!'

Festus consulted with his council and answered,

'You appealed to Caesar? To Caesar you shall go!'

The apostle was on his way to the capital of the empire, but he knew that his life was in the hands of someone higher than the Roman emperor.

Chapter 14
Paul's Journey of Faith

While Paul was waiting in Caesarea before being transported to Rome to appear before Nero, King Agrippa came to visit Festus. When he heard of Paul's case, he wanted to listen to the details of it first hand. As Paul stood before him, it was the fifth time he had been in court for the gospel. It must have been tempting to have minimized his testimony in order to gain worldly approval, but even though his reputation was despised by his own people, he remained true to the message of the One who had been despised and rejected for his salvation. He knew a God given strength in his own natural weakness and he was content to rely on that.

King Agrippa the Second had a greater understanding of Judaism than Festus. He knew Jewish history, but his own lifestyle and pedigree were scandalous. His great grandfather had caused the streets of Bethlehem to flow with blood when he had murdered every male child under the age of two, in an attempt to exterminate Jesus. His father, Herod Agrippa had killed James and imprisoned Peter. Then, after he had revelled in the flattering idolatry of the people of Tyre and Sidon who had worshipped him as a god, he had died in front of them after being eaten up by intestinal worms.

His own partner was called Bernice. She was not his wife but his sister. Even pagan Rome was shocked at the way this incestuous relationship was flaunted before the world. She had already gone to be the mistress of the emperor Vespasian and then of his son Titus, before returning to this debauched relationship with her own brother.

Now Paul stood before a decadent court, presided over by Agrippa. He had no defending council, but was told,

'You are permitted to speak for yourself.'

To the apostle this was another God given opportunity to confess his faith in Christ! He knew that the grace of God could save even a man like Agrippa if he would repent and turn to the Lord!

'I think myself happy King Agrippa because today I shall answer for myself before you concerning all the things of which I am accused by the Jews, especially because you are expert in all the customs and questions which have to do with the Jews. Therefore I beg you to hear me patiently.'

Reiterating the details of his own personal testimony, he explained how he had come to serve and be a witness for Christ. God's love had transformed him from being a hard man, to having a heart that was concerned for others. His defence before his accusers was to share the truth of the gospel and its confirmation by the resurrection of the Lord Jesus.

As soon as Paul had finished speaking, Festus interrupted and accused him of being absolutely insane. However, he calmly answered,

'I am not mad, most noble Festus, but speak the words of truth and reason, for the king before whom I also speak freely knows these things.'

Then making a personal application of the truths he had been sharing he turned to Agrippa and said,

'King Agrippa, do you believe the prophets?'

Without waiting for a reply, he went on,

'I know you do believe!'

Agrippa answered,

'You almost persuade me to become a Christian.'

Paul responded,

'Would to God that not only you, but also all who hear me today, might become almost and altogether such as I am, except for these chains!'

Then Agrippa said to Festus,

'This man might have been set free if he had not appealed to Caesar.'

Paul had been declared innocent, but in effect Agrippa had side stepped the challenge of the gospel. 'Almost persuaded' was not enough to save his own soul from eternal judgement.

Paul had courageously faced Agrippa, even after his own life had been threatened. He was living for a purpose beyond himself that conquered his fears. The message of eternity was in his heart.

Soon the day came when he was to set off as a prisoner to Rome. It was decided that they should sail to Italy and Paul was handed over to a Roman centurion who would be his custodian during the voyage. Doctor Luke and Aristarchus, the disciple who had been attacked by the crowds during the mission in Ephesus accompanied him. The centurion was a fair minded man called Julius. He was a soldier on detached duties, a bit like a cross between a prison warder and a military policeman. As a Roman citizen, Paul was treated comparatively well, but his trust was still in God alone.

He used every one of the little privileges he had to speak of Jesus Christ.

After the ship launched out, the journey was slow, because the weather was not good. In fact, the voyage very quickly became quite dangerous and as the sailors navigated around Crete, the vessel had to take shelter in a little bay called Fair Havens, on southern end of the island. The name may have sounded like a holiday resort, but it was no holiday for Paul, Luke and Aristarchus. They had not asked for their own comfort level to be the confirmation of their calling to be missionaries! Fair Havens did not offer enough protection for a winter anchorage and so the crew wanted to move on, but Paul warned Julius that it would be dangerous. The day of the Passover Feast had passed and so it would have been between September and October, a time when sea travel could be very hazardous. The centurion consulted the ship owner, who would have wanted as speedy a voyage as possible, because of the financial considerations. Then he consulted the helmsman of the vessel who encouraged him to launch out again. Accepting this advice, he ignored Paul's warning and they set sail as soon as there was a gentle southerly wind. It was only forty miles to the safe harbour of Pheonix and they considered it would be more suitable to stay there until the spring.

The wind had blown gently when they launched out, but appearances can be deceptive!

A hurricane swept in from the north east and the storm broke with such devastating power that the boat was in danger of sinking. The ships cargo was lost and the stars were hidden, so their navigation had gone too. The vessel was out of control as it tossed from one wave to the next under the blackness of the storm ridden sky. Even the experienced sailors despaired of their lives.

It's amazing the lengths people have to go to before they are prepared to listen!

Then in the middle of all of this, Paul had a word from the Lord!

'Do not be afraid Paul, you must be brought before Caesar and indeed God has granted you all those who sail with you!'

What a wonderful thing it is to hear God's Word in the midst of the storms of life.

As the ship careered through the water, it was driven towards the coastline of Malta. Luke described its erratic course with nautical detail. Fourteen nights had passed, they took soundings and recorded the depth as one hundred and twenty feet, then shortly afterwards it was ninety feet. They were aware that there was a real danger of being cast up on a rocky shoreline with considerable loss of life. The fearful sailors prayed! How often in moments of desperation, even the hardest hearts will recognise that there is something beyond the natural man and will cry out for God to help them.

The sailors prayed for the day to break; but it was still night.

Then they tried to escape. They tried to abandon the ship and save their own skins, but Paul's word stopped them. He told Julius, the centurion,

'Unless these men stay in the ship, you cannot be saved.'

This time Paul's word was recognised as having authority. His self control and consideration for others had given them a respect for his message.

The soldiers cut the ropes used to lower the dingy from the main vessel so that the sailors had to stay on board. When it was nearly daybreak, Paul encouraged everybody to eat a meal. They had been without nourishment for two weeks and because of this they were weak. Soon they would need all the strength they could muster; The ship was going to be lost and they would have to have to battle individually through the waves and on towards the shore.

There were two hundred and seventy six people on board and every one of these was important to God! Paul spoke again and assured them that none of them would lose their life. In a dangerous situation himself, he served God by caring for others.

After they had eaten, they threw the rest of the cargo into the sea, along with the anchors. Raising the mainsail they let the vessel be driven towards the shore, hoping that it would run on to the beach, but instead the ship hit a sandbank and the waves that crashed into the stern of the vessel broke it into pieces. The soldiers would have killed the prisoners, rather than face the consequences of having allowed them to escape, but the centurion forbade them to do this. He respected Paul and wanted to spare his life.

Another command was given for those who could swim to jump overboard and head for the shore. The rest were to take hold of a wooden board and drift in.

What a picture of life in this stormy world. How many lives Satan would shipwreck and destroy; families splintered and broken; but every person is precious to God!

The vessel of every physical body will perish, but there is a Savour of the soul who still gives His word of salvation today.

Those storm-tossed, ship-wrecked, sailors along with Paul, Luke, Aristarchus and every passenger on board, were all cast up on the shore of Malta and saved. God had been true to His word. In their kindness the islanders came out in the cold and rain and lit a fire in order to create some warmth. Paul took a bundle of sticks to put on the flames and immediately a viper from the bundle fixed on his arm with venomous intent.

Those who saw it immediately thought,

'No doubt this man is a murderer, whom though he has escaped the sea, yet justice does not allow to live.'

However, when Paul shook the serpent into the flames and the poison didn't do him any harm, they began to think he was a god!

The devil himself had originally attacked man in the guise of a serpent, bringing the poison of sin that polluted all of humanity. Here Paul's experience with the snake was a prophetic pointer to Satan's final destiny in hell. Paul's own life had been preserved through shipwreck and snakebite to share the message of salvation with the people of Malta.

He spent three months on the island, during which time God continued to use him to declare His word. His witness was confirmed by further miraculous signs. The father of Publius, the Roman governor of the island was very ill with dysentery. When Paul went and laid hands on him, he prayed and the disease immediately left him. As a result many of the other folk on the island who had various sicknesses came and were prayed for too. They all were healed.

After the winter had passed Paul, Luke and Aristarchus were ready to embark again. The Maltese people showed their respect by giving them gifts and other provisions.

These missionaries had honoured the Lord and the Lord had honoured them.

God had told Paul that he would stand before Caesar and soon they were to set sail again for the capital of the empire.

An Alexandrian merchant ship landed on the island, en route from Egypt to Italy, carrying grain. The figurehead on the ship was a model of the twin brothers Castor and Pollux, the sons of Zeus. In a pagan society these 'gods' were supposed to protect sailors. Paul had come out of religious hypocrisy but was now a prisoner among the idol worshipping servants of a foreign power. However he knew that the only true and living God was with him and really was able to keep him in the midst of every situation. Wherever he went he sought to witness for the Lord.

The ship sailed to Syracuse in Sicily and stayed there for three days. Tradition says that Paul planted a church there. From Syracuse they sailed across to Rhegium on the Italian mainland and then on up to Puteoli, which was the main port of Rome.

At Puteoli, Paul and his companions found some other Christians who offered them hospitality. Heaven will reward that little gesture of kindness and faith that has been recorded in scripture. They were able to fellowship together with them for a full week before moving on towards the capital.

Some of the Christians from Rome had heard from the Christians in Puteoli that the apostle Paul and his friends were coming and so they had travelled forty three miles along the Appian Way, to meet with them there. From the market town of Appii Forum, they travelled with them the thirteen miles to the Three Inns, a resting place on the way, where other believers joined with them. As this band of pilgrims went on the last thirty mile section of their journey together, they encouraged one another in their faith. Paul was strengthened and he thanked God for these unnamed brethren who had shared with him in this ministry for the Lord. To 'encourage' is literally 'to impart courage.' This is a precious service among the faithful.

Paul went to Rome strengthened to face the challenge ahead. When the party arrived there, Julius handed his charge over to the captain of the guard. His own duty was completed, but he would never forget the words and witness that he had heard and seen on the journey from Jerusalem to Rome. Perhaps it was because of the report he gave when he handed his prisoner over, that rather than being locked up, Paul was initially allowed to remain under open house arrest. Later, even though he was a Roman prisoner awaiting his trial before Nero, Paul invited the leaders of the Jewish community to come and visit him. When they gathered at the house where he was imprisoned, he told them,

'I have done nothing against our people, or the customs of our fathers... For the hope of Israel I am bound with this chain.'

Even though he was bound with a chain, he was not bound with bitterness. The true hope of Israel was not simply for a land of their own, free from an occupying army, but for the Messiah who would reign for eternity. The prophetic promises of His earthly kingdom spoke of an order of righteousness and fruitfulness. The last book of the bible speaks of a time when the Messiah will rule with a rod of iron.

This reign will last for a thousand years. Interestingly there have already been a number of counterfeits of this kingdom, not least, the diabolical promise of the Third Reich to reign for that time, after world war two. The increasing evidence of history fulfilling scriptural prophesy indicates that the day of the Lord's promised return is very near. The fact that the nation of Israel has returned to the promised land, after two thousand years of exile, is nothing less than a miracle.

The Bible does warn of another counterfeit leader who will appear in the last days and deceive many, but Paul's concern was to see his own flesh and blood coming to know the true Saviour. He was so passionately concerned about this, that he was willing to spiritually perish himself if his nation would receive Jesus. His heart desire and prayer to God for Israel was that they might be saved. Jesus Christ is still the Messiah, the Saviour from heaven sent as the true hope for the Children of Israel.

Paul spoke of the Kingdom of God and of the Lord Jesus, from the Law and the Prophets.

There had already been a Christian witness in Rome for some time. In his earlier letter to the believers, Paul had addressed people who were in Caesar's own household, as well as to men and women from across the empire who had gone to live in the capital. Following the outpouring of the Holy Spirit, the gospel would most likely have been taken back there by the Jews who had been in Jerusalem on the day of Pentecost, as well as by the Roman soldiers, who had been stationed in the city.

When the Jewish leaders spoke to Paul, they described the Christians as a 'sect that was being spoken against everywhere.'

Even though a truly Christian witness has brought blessing to people wherever it has been, the challenge of the gospel has always been opposed by those who would not acknowledge it's divine instigator.

Some of the leaders in the Jewish community in Rome accepted Paul's testimony and some disbelieved. For those who rejected the message, he quoted from Isaiah, referring to those who,

'Hearing you will hear and shall not understand and seeing you will see and not perceive;

for the hearts of this people have grown dull, ears are hard of hearing and their eyes they have closed.'

It was strong language and Paul made a very direct application of it. When he had challenged them in this way, he went on to say that he had been sent to the Gentiles who would hear the message. He had already written in his letter to the Roman church, speaking of God's work among the Gentiles and yet emphasising that the Lord had not finished with the people of Israel. He had warned the Gentile believers not to become proud of their own privileged position as Christians, or bigoted against the Jews. This chosen nation of Israel was the root of the tree into which the Gentiles had been grafted. The religious branches of dead Jewish practice had been lopped off, so that the Gentile Christians could be brought in. However the promises that God had given to the patriarchs with whom He had made a covenant, would still be kept! The Children of Israel who had honoured the Lord by their faith and obedience to His word would see His promises outworked.

When the full compliment of Gentile believers had come to Christ, Paul declared that,

'All Israel would be saved.'

But he also warned that ,

'They are not all Israel, who are of Israel.'

Isaiah the prophet had promised Israel that,

'A Deliverer will come out of Zion and He will turn away ungodliness from Jacob.'

This would be God's covenant with them when He took away their sin.

It was not merely having the right genetic line that would produce a spiritual inheritance; this inheritance was for those who heard and humbly received the promises of God's Word and followed His instruction.

Paul's warnings about unbelief and disobedience were not merely for those under the Old Covenant, he warned the Gentile believers under the New Covenant as well.

While under house arrest, he stayed in the place he had rented and preached about the Kingdom of God for the next two years.

This message about God who willingly came in humility from a heavenly throne to live among a sinful people who would crucify Him, was very different to any kingdom that the people of Rome knew about.

This gospel that was for the Jew first and then for the Gentile, is still the message of salvation to all.

When the Lord faced His own death, He promised that He would return again for those who had accepted Him into their own life.

The Kingdom of God is within the heart of every true believer as they live under the authority of King Jesus. When He comes back as King of Kings, He will fulfil every remaining detail of His promises to the prophets of Israel and then He will reign over a new heavens and a new earth for all eternity.

Paul had been called to be an apostle, one who was sent with a message that was far more significant than man's wisdom could bring. It had been delivered in God given power.

His ministry in Rome consisted of two periods in prison, punctuated by a time of freedom, during which he revisited and encouraged many of the churches he had planted. In July 64AD the city was almost destroyed by fire and Nero accused the Christians of arson. Paul's second and final prison term in Rome was not under house arrest, but chained in isolation in the Mamertime jail. His earthly journey had nearly finished, but he was looking up to heaven and sharing a message that is still the same today and will be until the Lord returns in great power and glory.

Chapter 15
God's Ultimate Purpose

From God's perspective, the Acts of the Holy Spirit are followed by the Revelation of Jesus Christ. John the apostle received an angelic unveiling of this vision to bring to the church.

By about 95AD, John as an old man, was still ministering by the power of the Holy Spirit to the churches in and around Ephesus. He had cared for the believers and strengthened them in their faith with a prophetic ministry that brought both challenge and encouragement. His forthright message of salvation through Christ alone had confronted both pagan deities and emperor worship. The declaration of the message of the Kingdom of God brought spiritual and political conflict and as a result, John was arrested and deported to Patmos. This volcanic island in the Aegean sea, ten miles long and six miles wide, was used as a Roman prison. It was situated about thirty five miles off the south-western coast of Asia Minor, where the apostle Paul had seen the birth and growth of the various Christian churches.

Dr Luke had kept a written account of all that he had seen and heard following the day of Pentecost. The apostle John had been an elder in the church in Ephesus. Now he received a personal revelation by angelic messenger of God's purpose to unveil the full and eternal reign of His Son. Almighty God had used the first disciples and apostles in a special way, but then the Holy Spirit continued to move in many lives to build the church of Christ in a sinful world.

In AD 68, after Nero had committed suicide, Vespasian the general who was leading the attack against the city of Jerusalem, was recalled to Rome to become the new emperor. His son Titus took charge of the invading army.

Flavius Josephus, was a Jew who had deserted his own people and joined with the Romans. He gave an eye witness account of the horrific destruction of the temple in AD70. Amid the genocide of the invasion, the Temple where the nation had worshipped God for centuries, was burnt to the ground. Thousands were killed in the carnage that followed and others were deported from their own land into positions of slave labour across the empire.

During His earthly ministry one brief generation earlier, Jesus had wept over Jerusalem and described in prophetic detail all that would happen.

One Sunday during his captivity on the island of Patmos, John was full of the Holy Spirit. Suddenly Jesus revealed Himself to him in the way that was not dissimilar to the vision the apostle Paul had been given on the Damascus road. He heard a voice behind him that spoke with the resonant authority of a trumpet call and commissioned him to write to the churches in Asia Minor. The message was of eternal significance.

When he looked to see who was speaking he saw the Son of Man, the risen Saviour, the Lord Jesus, standing in majesty, radiant with a glorious authority, declaring the final outworking of history.

Under the Romans, Asia Minor had been divided up into seven postal districts with a key city in the centre of each one. John's circular letter was addressed to each of these. However his message was not simply for their local concern. It had a prophetic significance that was for the world-wide church throughout time.

To the church at Ephesus he wrote,

'I know your works, your labour, your patience and that you cannot bear those who are evil. You have tested those who say they are apostles and are not and have found them liars. You have persevered and have patience and have laboured for My Names sake and have not become weary. Nevertheless I have this against you, that you have left your first love. Remember therefore from where you have fallen; repent and do the first works, or else I will come quickly and remove your lamp stand from its place. But you do have this; you hate the deeds of the Nicolaitans, which I also hate.

He who has an ear, let him hear what the Spirit says to the churches.

To him who overcomes I will give to eat from the tree of life, which is in the Paradise of God.'

The Nicolatians followed Nicolas, a deacon in the early church who had turned from the Lord and led people into moral depravity. John had given a strong prophetic warning to the church, but the devil still sought to deviate people from a pure faith.

False leaders have turned many away from Christ throughout history and led people back into bondage to Satan. Lucifer, the devil, was the very instigator of this rebellion against God and with this purpose as his motive, he has deceived people throughout the generations. In the last days his deceptions will become stronger and even more frequent. The true hope of deliverance from deception is found in Christ alone.

By AD 381 the Ephesian church had become wealthy and comfortable. They called the surrounding churches to the Council of Ephesus and honoured Mary as the mother of God. This was a step nearer to the pagan deities, worshipped by the surrounding nations. Shortly afterwards there were violent earthquakes in the area and the harbour silted up. As a result commercial trade was unable to continue and the people moved away from the city. Centuries later Islam swept in by military conquest. Tragically the lampstand of the Christian witness had already been removed and the church had died. The so called Christian Crusades of the middle ages, that sent armies marching towards Jerusalem, were motivated by religious pride and political intention, not by love for Christ.

To the church at Smyrna, John wrote,

'I know your works, tribulation and poverty,(but you are rich!) and I know the blasphemy of those who say they are Jews and are not, but are a synagogue of Satan. Do not fear any of those things which you are about to suffer. Indeed the devil is about to throw some of you into prison, that you may be tested and some of you will have tribulation for three days. Be faithful unto death and I will give you the crown of life.

He who has an ear, let him hear what the Spirit says to the churches. He who overcomes shall not be hurt by the second death.'

The first death was physical, the second death was spiritual. The challenge was for individuals to be willing to lay down their lives for God. This call was to not some practise of twisted, religious masochism, but to honour the Lord and be example of His love and righteousness, even to those who despised His Name. Polycarp, the bishop or shepherd of the church in Smyrna had been converted under the ministry of the apostle John. Around AD160 as an old man of eighty six he was challenged to deny his faith or be burnt to death. He chose to be martyred for Christ.

Smyrna is now called Izmir and has a small Christian witness that is growing. The Bible has been translated into the modern Turkish language and in the twenty-first century, increasing numbers of people living in and around the area are searching through the Scriptures and discovering who Jesus really is.

Pergamos was the regional capital city where the cult of Caesar worship built its first temple in Asia Minor. The uniting of political and religious power in the worship of a man, has always been a dangerous combination that needs to be guarded against.

In Pergamos there was a medical school associated with the temple of Zeus. Pergamos was the headquarters for a variety of demonized forms of worship to pagan gods. Balaam had been a prophet in the Old Testament who had tried to sell his prophetic gifting in order to bring the Children of Israel into idolatry and sexual sin. These conditions are reflected in the world today!

Antipas, the pastor of the church in Pergamos, had been burnt to death for remaining faithful to the gospel. John addressed the believers who still worshipped there,

'I know your works and where you dwell; where Satan's throne is!-You hold fast to My Name. You did not deny my faith even in the days in which Antipas, my faithful martyr, was killed among you, where Satan dwells. But I have a few things against you because you have there those who hold to the doctrine of Balaam. He taught Balak to put a stumbling block before the Children of Israel, to eat things sacrificed to idols and to commit sexual immorality. You also had those who hold to the doctrine of the Nicolaitans, which I hate! Repent or else I will come to you quickly and fight against them with the sword of my mouth.

He who has an ear let him hear what the spirit says to the churches.'

However the corrective challenge of the message did have some encouragement for the believers who remained faithful.

'To him who overcomes, I will give some of the hidden manna to eat. I will give him a white stone and on the stone a new name written which no one knows except him who receives it.'

John then included in his circular letter, instructions for the church in Thyatira. In each of the letters to the churches, he had made clear that the authority behind what he was writing was that of the Lord Himself.

'The Son of God who has eyes like a flame of fire and feet like fine brass says:-

I know your works, love, service, faith and your patience.

As for your works, the last are more than the first. Nevertheless I have a few things against you, because you allow that woman Jezebel, who calls herself a prophetess, to teach and seduce my servants to commit sexual immorality and eat things sacrificed to idols. I gave her time to repent of her sexual immorality and she did not repent. Indeed I will cast her into a sickbed and those who commit adultery with her, into great tribulation, unless they repent of their deeds. I will kill her children with death and all the churches shall know that I am He who searches the minds and hearts. I will give each one of you according to your works. Now to you and the rest in Thyatira who do not have this doctrine and who have not known Satan's depths, I will not burden you further.

Hold fast what you have till I come. To him who overcomes and keeps my works to the end I will give power over the nations, I also received from My Father and I will give him the morning star. He shall rule them with a rod of iron. They shall be dashed in pieces like the potters vessel.

He who has an ear, let him hear what the Spirit says to the churches.

The name Jezebel was more probably descriptive of the character of this particular woman in the assembly, rather than being her actual name. The original Jezebel had married King Ahab of Israel around 880 BC in what was basically a political alliance with Tyre and Sidon. She had imported her corrupt and decadent religion into the land. Instead of worshipping Yahweh, the true God, she had continued to worship the false Baal, the pagan god of Samaria. This included the horrific practice that Elijah had challenged the people over on Mount Carmel. The heaven sent fire of God confirmed His judgment on Baal worship. Jezebel, who had practised and brought the vile belief system into the nation, was discredited. Her name became synonymous with profane religion.

These messages from the Lord, given through John, had to be spiritually discerned.

Spiritual discernment is probably more necessary today than it was even in the days both of Elijah and the apostle John! Profane religion practised under the guise of respectability is still obnoxious to God.

The word addressed to the church in Sardis challenged cultural Christianity in a conclave of comparative material and social security, where faith was merely nominal. This challenge also is still very, very relevant in society today. John wrote to Sardis,

'I know your works that you have a name that you are alive, but you are dead. Be watchful and strengthen the things which remain, that are ready to die, for I have not found your works perfect before God. Remember therefore what you have received and heard; hold fast to it and repent! If you will not watch, I will come upon you as a thief and you will not know what hour I will come upon you. You have a few names, even in Sardis who have not defiled their garments and they shall walk with me in white, for they are worthy. He who overcomes shall be clothed in white garments and I will not blot his name out of the Book of Life, but I will confess his name before My Father and before His angels.

He who has an ear let him hear what the Spirit says to the churches.'

The letter conveyed a poetic, prophetic, personal challenge to have a living relationship with God.

The words to the Philadelphian church again identified their author,

'These things says He who is holy, He who is true; He who holds the key of David, He who opens and no one shuts and shuts and no one opens.'

The word of the Lord to this church was one of encouragement.

'I know your works. See, I have set before you an open door and no one can shut it; for you have a little strength, have kept My Word and have not denied My Name. Indeed, I will make those of the synagogue of Satan who say they are Jews and are not, but lie- indeed I will make them come and worship at your feet and know that I have loved you. Because you have kept my command to persevere, I will also keep you from the hour of trial that shall come upon the whole world, to test those who dwell on the earth. Behold, I am coming quickly! Hold fast what you have, that no one may take your crown. He who overcomes, I will make a pillar in the temple of My God and he shall go out no more. I will write on him the name of the city of My God, the New Jerusalem, which comes down out of heaven from My God. I will write on him My new name.

He who has an ear let him hear what the Spirit says to the churches.'

The name 'Philadelphia' meant 'brotherly love' and the love of Christ that held the church together in a city subject to repeated earthquakes, made it a precious witness to the unchanging love of God in a shaking world.

To the Laodicean church, the last of the seven that John addressed, came perhaps the greatest challenge of all.

'The One who was the Amen, the faithful and true witness, the Beginning of the creation of God, said,

'I know your works, that you are neither cold nor hot. I could wish you were cold or hot. So then, because you are lukewarm and neither cold not hot, I will vomit you out of My mouth.'

Because you say, 'I am rich, have become wealthy and have need of nothing and because you do not know that you are wretched, miserable, poor, blind and naked, I counsel you to buy from me gold refined in the fire, that you may be rich and white garments that you may be clothed, that the shame of your nakedness may not be revealed. Anoint your eyes with eye salve, that you may see. As many as I love, I rebuke and chasten. Therefore be zealous and repent. Behold I stand at the door and knock. If anyone hears My voice and opens the door, I will come in to him and dine with him and he with Me. To him who overcomes, I will grant to sit with me on my throne, as I overcame and sat down with My Father on His throne.

He who has an ear, let him hear what the Spirit says to the churches.'

Laodicea was a city famous for its banking system, its clothes made of black wool and its medicinal eye salve. However, it's water supply was insipid after being piped in from hot water springs some distance away. The population there thought they were wealthy, well dressed and far sighted, but in fact they were spiritually poor, needed to be dressed in the white robes of righteousness and be given clear spiritual vision. Instead of fellowship with them being like a drink of pure, clear, refreshing water, it was sickening. God's Word to the Laodicean church was perhaps the strongest of all.

It has been suggested that the warnings given to these seven congregations have been particularly relevant to church life in set periods of history. Some have applied the challenge given to the Laodiceans to much of western Christianity today. Even though the message to each of the chosen churches that John addressed seemed to be appropriate to the conduct of the world wide church during specific periods of time, the challenge given to all of them is relevant to the Christian witness in the world today.

When he was imprisoned on Patmos, John was given an understanding of the purposes that the Lord had for His people in the future. He saw his Saviour reigning as the Lamb upon the throne and he heard the voices of multitudes of the saints raised in heavenly worship. His own hope was not in the things of this world, but in the God of eternity. He knew that the Lord was with him, even in his isolation. As he wrote his letters addressing the various situations across the region of Asia Minor, God was speaking through him and challenging the discouragement, the materialism, the apathy, the selfishness, the carnality and spiritual deception that would attack the church until Jesus returned.

In his revelation to the seven churches, John used the code name of 'Babylon' to describe a spiritual authority that was corrupt and false. The name of Babylon had been used in a descriptive way throughout scripture, following the construction of the Tower of Babel, when men tried to build a city specifically for occult practices in an endeavour to reach God. At the time that John wrote, the name Babylon was synonymous with the power of Rome, where Caesar claimed to be divine.

With prophetic insight into the last days of history the apostle heard a voice from heaven saying,

'Come out of her my people, lest you share in her sins and lest you receive of her plagues.'

The warnings that were given to the churches in Asia Minor, are for today.

Scripture warns that in the last days there will be a counterfeit church made of an amalgam of spiritual practises. All of these will have been inspired by Satan, the great deceiver, in his endeavour to turn people away from a personal relationship with the true Christ.

May every gathering of Christian believers clearly hear what the Spirit is saying to the churches today! This alone is how the life of the Lord can be revealed.

The promised Holy Spirit still gives divine power to keep His people pure and to live in the centre of God's purpose!

Throughout the conflicts of history and society, salvation has valued and imparted the values of Christ to every repentant sinner. But Almighty God intends to do more! Satan is going to be judged and a new creation will be brought into being. Jesus, the Son of the Living God, is coming to reign in divine majesty as King of Kings and Lord of Lords for all of eternity. This full and eternal revelation of the risen Saviour, clothed in majesty and power is soon to happen. As the head of His church, Jesus will be sovereign over a new creation.

In the way that the Lord had given prophetic warning of the fall of Jerusalem in AD70, John in Revelation, by the inspiration of the Holy Spirit gives prophetic warning of the final conflicts of history before Christ returns to earth.

The present call to holy living in a sinful world is exemplified by Christian witnesses throughout history who 'loved not their lives unto death.'

'They overcame the accuser of the brethren by the Blood of the Lamb and the word of their testimony.'

Heaven was their home!

The Lord Jesus had not only promised the Holy Spirit to every true believer, He had promised His disciples that He would prepare a place where they would be with Him for eternity.

At the end of John's revelation, he saw a heavenly city, a place where there were no more tears, no more death, no sorrow or crying and no pain, but everything made new and perfect. In this new creation, all of the universe will unite in praise to God. The heavens and the earth will be filled with the glory of the Lord. The musical harmony of worship will resound through every heart and in every life. The perfect splendour of all of this, in fellowship with His Son, has been God's purpose from the very beginning.

This will be made possible because Almighty God is going to reveal His final judgment against Lucifer. He will be cast into the bottomless pit of hell, never to tempt and torment again; banished for all of eternity. At that final judgment those who have followed Satan will go to be with him, but those who have followed the Lord Jesus Christ will reign with Him in a kingdom that will know no end!

The true church is comprised of people from every land and nation from throughout history who have known salvation in Christ alone. Even the Godly people from the Old Covenant will be saved because of the work of Calvary. They too will rejoice with the One who Paul said had been crucified from the foundation of the earth. This has been God's intention from the very beginning and He is still calling men and women to be a part of it while time remains. Whosoever will may come!

Conclusion

One day when Jesus was sitting on the Mount of Olives, His disciples came and asked Him to tell them of the signs that would indicate that the present world system was drawing to a close.

The very first thing Jesus spoke of was spiritual deception. The heart-response of many believers would become cold and many would fall away from a true faith in Christ. At the same time there would be many others claiming to be God's anointed messenger. We don't have to listen for long to what is going on in the world to be made aware of the multiplicity of false messiahs today! Not only would there be a false spirituality and a falling away from the truth, but true disciples of the Lord Jesus would face increasing persecution. The martyrdom of Christians is far more prolific today than it was even in the days of Nero. More Christian believers have been martyred since the beginning of twentieth century than in all of the rest of previous history put together. Take note of what is happening across the nations of the earth today.

One of the spiritual signs pointing towards the return of the Lord to this earth will be the evidence of increased ethnic and military conflict. There will be warlike propaganda. The last century has had two world wars and numerous international confrontations. The early years of this present century have already been steeped in violence.

Another sign of the Lord's return will be that of an increase in diseases and natural disasters, pandemics, famines, earthquakes.

The apostle Paul had said that,

'The whole creation groans and labours with birth pangs together until now.'

Listen to the news!

There will be cosmic signs indicating the proximity of the second coming of Christ.

The sun and moon will be darkened, stars will fall. The heavens will shake. Whether this will be caused by interplanetary conflict or not, is not specified.

Politics has always been a dirty game, but in the last days it will become far more corrupt in its attempt to manipulate people and nations towards a Godless end. Many of the politicians themselves will be unaware that they are mere pawns in the cosmic outworking of history.

The political situation in the middle east will become increasingly inflamed. A false peace treaty will be made and then broken. The prophet Zechariah warned in the sixth century BC of a day before the Lord finally returns when Jerusalem will be surrounded by an attacking United Nation's army. The events that occurred in AD 70 were only a foretaste of what will happen in the very last days.

There will be financial signs indicating the closeness of Christ's return.

Trade will not be allowed without the 'mark of the beast' or the number of his name being on the forehead or hand of the people involved. John in his Revelation spoke of this diabolical spiritual power controlling a world wide currency system in order to dominate peoples behaviour for his own ends.

A world currency, a world army and a world religion are part of the devil's plan to counterfeit God's Kingdom. These things are approaching even now and are unrecognised by many.

Listen to the news! The days are short!

To echo the words of the people on the day of Pentecost,

'What should we do in the light of these things?'

Jesus Christ gives us God's answer.

'Look up, for the coming of the Lord is at hand!'

As the early disciples looked for the coming Kingdom of God they themselves did what was to hand!

They knew the joy of the Lord as their strength because they had a glorious hope set before them. Jesus Christ will still give that hope to all who receive Him as their Saviour.

The climactic end of world history is not the end for the true Believer: it is merely the introduction to a greater glory! The Saviour, who promised His disciples the empowering of the Holy Spirit, promised to return personally. Jesus is coming to reign and we shall be with Him!

May we be about the Master's business today!

Scriptural References

This narrative is taken from the biblical records referred to in brackets after each separate chapter. The further Scriptural references are given for direct quotes from the Bible.

Chapter 1 (drawn from Acts chapters 1-2.)
Acts1v11, 1Kings18v21, Acts2v17, Acts2v40, Luke22v19-20.

Chapter 2 (drawn from Acts chapters 3-4v31.)
Luke19v46, Isaiah56v7, Luke19v46, Acts3v4, Acts3v6, Acts3v12, Acts3v14-15, Acts2v22, Isaiah53v3-5, Acts4v8-10, Acts4v12, Acts4v19-20, Acts4v25-26, Acts4v28, Hebrews12v26-27, Luke6v47-49, John13v34-35

Chapter 3 (drawn from Acts chapters 4v32-5v32.)
Acts5v3-4, Acts 5v9, Psalm111v10, Acts 5v20, Acts5v29, Matthew10v22, Matthew16v18, Psalm 116v15, Revelation 12v11

Chapter 4. (drawn from Acts chapters 5v33-7v60.)
Genesis12v1-4, Acts7v51-52, Acts7v59-60, Isaiah66v2, Acts 7v60, Luke23v34

Chapter 5 (drawn from Acts chapter 8v1-40.)
John 4v7, John 4v10, John 4v16, John 4v22, John 4v37, John 8v20-21, John 8v31, John1v29, John 8v36-37

Chapter 6 (drawn from Acts chapter 9.)
John 14v6, Acts 9v6, Acts9v17

Chapter 7 (drawn from Acts chapters10v1-12v24.)
Matthew16v13, Matthew 16v16, 1Peter2v4-7, Matthew 16v22 , Matthew26v34, Luke22v33-34, John21v5-6, John21 v15-17, Acts 9v34, Acts9v40, Acts 10v15, Acts10v20, Acts10v34-36, Acts12v7-8, Luke17v6, Matt17v20

Chapter 8 (drawn from Acts chapters 9v25-13.)
Luke24v49, Acts9v15, Acts13v30, Acts10 v47

Chapters 9 (drawn from Acts chapters 14-15v21.)
Acts14v10, Acts14v22

Chapter 10 (drawn from Acts chapters 15v21-17v15.)
Acts16v17, Acts16v28-30, Acts17v3, 1Thessalonians1v8-9,
1Thessalonians5v2
Chapter 11 (drawn from Acts chapters 17v16-18v23.)
1Corinthians1v24, Luke1v46, 1Corinthians6v8-11
Chapter 12 (drawn from Acts chapters18v24-19v41.)
Acts19v2, 1Corinthians3v3-6, 1Corinthians1v12, 1Corithians1v27,
Acts19v13, Acts19v15, Acts19v20, Acts19v28, Ephesians3v8 ,
Ephesians6v12-18
Chapter 13 (drawn from Acts chapters 20v1-26v32.)
Matthew22v37-39, Romans13v8, Acts 20v10, Philippians 1v21,
Acts20v18-22, Acts 20v26-30, Acts21v13, Acts22v22, Acts22v28 ,
Acts23v3, Acts23v11, Acts24v25, Acts25v11-12
Chapter 14 (drawn from Acts chapters 26v32- 28v31.)
Acts26v1-4, Acts26v25-28, Act26v29, Acts 26v32, Acts27v23-24 ,
Acts27v31, Acts28v4, Acts28v17&20, Acts28v26-27,
Romans11v26, Romans9v6
Chapter 15 (drawn from Revelation chapters1v1-3v22.)
Revelation 2v2-29, Revelation3v1-22, Revelation18v4,
Revelation12v11.
Conclusion
(Revelation 13 v16-18), (Zechariah14v1-9)
The above bracketed Scriptures are referred to but not quoted in
the chapter.
Romans8v22.